A Hero Behind Every Tree

The Non-Technical Reasons Your
IT Investments Fail

Learn from our mistakes so
you don't have to make them!

Steve Caudll

Russell
Mullen

Editing and layout by Christa Ayer of One Hundred Acres Consulting
www.onehundredacres.com

Published in the United States by Dacoda Projects, Virginia

www.dacoda.us

ISBN: 978-0-578-00405-1

Printed in the United States of America

First Edition

Table of Contents

Table of Figures

Introduction

Somewhere in a file cabinet or an overhead bin a cape and tights are neatly folded, waiting. They are waiting for the inevitable disaster, looming deadline, or last-minute crisis when an otherwise mild-mannered IT team member will don the hero uniform, swoop in, and save your project from certain doom. You hope that your hero is faster than a speeding requirement, more powerful than a team of consultants, and able to leap tall deadlines in a single bound, but you are never quite sure.

> *By the time you call for a hero, you have a technical problem — or several technical problems. However, you need a hero because of a non-technical failure earlier in the project.*

By the time you call for a hero, you have a technical problem — or several technical problems. However, you need a hero because of a non-technical failure earlier in the project. This book details ten non-technical issues providing practical advice and tools to address each of them. If you would like to relieve your heroes of the stress of saving the world time and again, you must address the non-technical issues common to IT projects and chief among them is the mindset that heroism is necessary to a successful IT project. The story below illustrates just how difficult it can be to change that mindset.

Why Write this Book?

It was a lovely day as we boarded the bus that would take us to headquarters for the celebration. I was with the project manager and technical lead of a major track — one of the chunks of work — of a huge (as in hundreds of millions of dollars) multi-year project. We were going to celebrate because one of the other tracks was "going live" at two locations. Not only did these locations represent a significant percentage of the business affected by the project, but this particular piece of work had been completed on-time and on-budget. There was reason to celebrate.

We filed into the headquarters' auditorium to smiles, back slapping and handshakes from the large audience of company staff. Live video feeds from the two "live" locations showed jubilant team members sharing waves and thumbs up with each other, us, and the rest of our audience. The lights dimmed and we listened to division presidents, operations executives, and senior team members praising the team. More work remained, but this was a time to congratulate those who had worked so hard to ensure success.

I took note of one particular speech. The speaker praised the many long hours and sometimes extraordinary effort, but reminded the audience that this kind of heroism was not sustainable. Besides, they had learned enough bringing these locations online that they could now implement other locations without the need for heroic long hours and super-human effort.

This was good news. Rarely does an organization take on a project of this scale and deliver as promised. Even more rarely do they recognize that heroes burn out quickly and long projects cannot rely on heroism for success. For a moment, my confidence in the team and leadership jumped significantly — but only for a moment. On the video feeds, I could see posters showing new users how to get help and encouraging them to learn the new system. The main character on the poster looked strikingly like a super-hero. Heroism was not only praised by almost every speaker at the celebration, but had been iconized on the project materials.

After the presentations, we gathered in the cafeteria for cake and coffee. The stories being told — the resulting folklore being created — were of heroic events. Those people most appreciated were the ones with bags under their eyes for lack of sleep. Groups formed around both the leaders and the heroes to exchange a handshake and a brief word of encouragement. The warning about heroism as a non-sustainable strategy was forgotten minutes after the words had been uttered.

It's a valid warning though. Heroism is unsustainable, and projects that rely on it can quickly turn from early success to overall failure. It was good to hear that the project team had overcome enough of these patterns to deliver on-time and on-budget, but the pattern of

Heroism is unsustainable, and projects that rely on it can quickly turn from early success to overall failure.

behavior that will ultimately lead to "hero burn out" looms over the rest of the project. When the heroes are gone, will the next track still be as successful? It's hard to tell.

Overcoming Newtonian Forces

That's what this book is about: showing how heroism and other patterns of behavior affect the overall success (or failure) of a project. For many years, Russ and I have been giving seminars and workshops on systems thinking, project methodology, risk management, requirements analysis, and the like. Our focus is always on low-cost, practical, and pragmatic tools and techniques designed around the non-technical problems of IT projects.

We address issues like promising more than you can deliver, figuring out what will go wrong before it does, and handling ambiguity. We share various tools and teach techniques that have helped us overcome failure. Our main jobs revolve around delivering IT systems, but we have enjoyed connecting with others in our field a few times a year through teaching.

We have a large archive of presentations, in-class exercises, and handouts that supplement our in-person presentations. Since the beginning, more than ten years ago, workshop and seminar attendees have asked if and when we will commit our presentations to writing in book form. For the first few years, we were still refining the message, learning new lessons on our own projects — and from others — and it was easy to delay writing while our thoughts matured. Then, we became too busy. Serving clients, training our own team, and traveling the globe left little time to do a proper job of putting our thoughts on paper. More recently, we have been full of good intentions, but, frankly, unwilling to put forth the effort, and our experience has been available only to those several hundred who attend our seminars each year.

Another road-block to writing a book has been deciding on what topic we should write. My background is technical: software development, analysis, and architecture and I have moved to oversight and executive management. Russ, while also originally a developer, has gravitated toward task-, project-, and risk-management. Between us is more than 40 years of experience — not just one year repeated forty times, but an almost unique amount of variation in project size, problem domain, market segment, and approach. With our broad background we have encountered a wide range of problems affecting IT projects. So, in addition to Newtonian forces — objects at rest stay at rest — that have hindered our writing, we have been faced with indecision about which problems and solutions to bring to a wider audience.

Then I attended the project celebration where heroism was on one hand discredited and on the other embraced. Several months ago, Russ and I gave a presentation on exactly this topic and got an overwhelming response. Finally we had both the motivation and the material; thus, this book.

Who are the Real Heroes?

You might ask what we have against heroes that would cause us to run out and start writing. Most of the project heroes we have encountered are great people, outstanding individuals, and the top contributors; however, they are heroes because someone — sometimes they themselves — made a mistake. There was some mismanaged situation that required them to "save the day."

At the go-live celebration did we praise the discipline that ensured the project came in on time? Did we tell stories of the teams that were able to work a normal work day for the duration of the project? No,

> *Most of the project heroes we have encountered are great people, outstanding individuals, and the top contributors; however, they are heroes because someone — sometimes they themselves — made a mistake. There was some mismanaged situation that required them to "save the day."*

we celebrated the extraordinary effort required to make up for some kind of miscalculation or error, and the people who had to work overtime to make up for it. This is the sad state of IT projects today, and even this project's success might turn out to be short-lived.

It is difficult to face the harsh reality that, on one of the best managed and controlled projects of my career, we are still failing to address the non-technical problems that have haunted IT projects since the code-and-go days of software development and the nightmarish wiring closets of early networking. Those non-technical causes of project failure that seem so difficult to recognize and purge from our organizations, and that contribute to something we call "hero syndrome," are the focus of this book.

Who Should Read this Book?

Russ and I are both IT guys, but we are also executives and understand clearly the need to get an adequate return on project investments. While what we say will be all too familiar to technicians and IT project managers, it is our hope that this text can be appreciated and understood by managers and executives who may not be part of a technology organization, but have to implement — or survive — IT projects or make investment decisions that include a technical or systems component.

When I studied for my MBA, the required systems management course covered much technical ground, but did not help executives make decisions about IT systems or know how to effectively manage projects with a technology component. It is our hope that this text fills at least some of that void by providing practical experience and advice. As we'll remind you throughout the book, in the end, the executive is responsible for the investment.

You don't have to be an executive, however, to come away from this book with something useful. If you are an IT project manager, developer, QA professional, or otherwise engaged in an IT project, I can say with some confidence that your project suffers from more than one of the issues we will discuss. I'm going to hold the executive rank responsible, but in turn they will hold IT managers responsible. Whatever role you play in a project, this is your chance to see the issues clearly and take steps to eradicate these behaviors from your part of the effort.

Russ writes: *Steve's comments about the praise and attention that is often heaped on heroes resonates with me as the right kind of attitude about exactly the wrong course of action.*

Something I read very early in my project management career went something like this:

"The best project managers are not the ones who go on vacation and are missed five minutes after they walk out the door, and then return a week later to find that the entire project has stagnated, gone astray, or completely fallen into disaster without their expert guidance. No, the best project manager is the one who leaves for vacation and nobody notices. Work continues, deadlines are met, and set-backs are dealt with and resolved, all without drama."

> *In applying this philosophy to every project I manage, I'm often chagrined at the lack of excitement surrounding my projects when they go exactly according to plan, with no drama and no emergencies, while the participants in projects that are hauled back from the brink of disaster are lauded for their super-human efforts.*

There's a synonymous phrase for indispensability that hardware folks will recognize as something to be avoided wherever possible: "single point of failure." Not being missed for a week doesn't mean you're unnecessary. It means you deliberately planned and prepared for your absence so, not only did the planned work get done, but even if something unexpected came up, it could be properly resolved. Planning for these kinds of issues, expected or unexpected, is a huge part of project management.

In applying this philosophy to every project I manage, I'm often chagrined at the lack of excitement surrounding my projects when they go exactly according to plan, with no drama and no emergencies, while the participants in projects that are hauled back from the brink of disaster are lauded for their super-human efforts. I've learned that often the personal satisfaction gained from guiding a project to the finish is praise enough. However, I sincerely (and maybe a little selfishly) hope that after reading *this book, managers and executives will take note of those on their staff who get the job done successfully without the need for a 24x7 presence, ingesting nuclear bombs, or warping the time-space continuum.*

Layout and Suggestions for Use

I hope you find this book to be an easy read and I hope you will read it straight through. For those who are looking for a different approach, you will find the material falls into four sections:

- Chapters 1 through 3 are introductory and explain more about the problem of heroism, our approach and a summary of our picks of the top-ten non-technical issues that plague IT projects. These chapters provide practical tools, but if you are in a hurry, you can skip them and return later to pick-up the tools.

- Chapters 4 through 13 address each of the top-ten issues individually. You can read them in any order. Many of the issues are related to others and we have included references to the specific chapters where appropriate to guide your reading.

- Chapter 14 summarizes the tools introduced in the preceding chapters and wraps up the main content. Use this chapter as a quick reference to the tools and the framework into which they fit.

- Appendix A fills the gap of tools we did not introduce in the main body of the book for those interested in seeing how we handle both technical and non-technical content. It is completely optional and necessarily brief. Both Appendix A and the bibliography can guide you to further work or reading if you want to explore supplementary and complementary material.

For those interested in using this book in a classroom or other group workout setting (see chapter 9). I suggest assigning the introduction and chapters 1 through 3 as pre-read material and discuss the concept, tool rules and top-ten list in an introductory session.

Then, discuss one or more of the ten issues from chapters 4 through 13 during the remaining sessions. I have found that students bring their own stories and may have their own tools which can be discussed and evaluated by the group.

I suggest time be allotted to practice with the tools in small teams using real projects or case-studies relevant to the group. Note that the number and difficulty of the tools varies by chapter so it might take some experimentation to fit practical exercises into your allotted time. The rules from chapter 2 apply to all of our tools which means no materials need be prepared in advance. To use the tools, all you will need are paper and pencils or a white board and markers.

We are eager to assist you in using this material for a good work-out or as part of formal training, please send your questions to the email addresses in the author biographies in the back of the book.

Protecting the Innocent

Both Russ and I are storytellers. You will find this book full of stories from our adventures with companies large and small and projects of many different types. After so many years in IT systems, consulting, and management, we don't need to fabricate scenarios to make a point; however, we also don't want to embarrass past or current clients. Companies usually hire consultants when things are going poorly, not when they are going well; so, we have many tales of disaster, mismanagement, and error.

The stories in this book are fiction only in that we have changed names, locations, and other identifying features that are not particularly germane to the story to prevent anyone familiar with our client list from putting the pieces together. Many of our leading characters learned from their mistakes and have gone on to greater success than we could have imagined. Some have not. We prefer to let them tell their own stories. So, in ours, we have kept them as anonymous as possible.

A Word about Voice

You probably noticed that the main voice in this book belongs to Steve. Russ and I write very much as we speak when we give seminars together. I ramble on, and Russ adds timely examples and zeroes in on key concepts. The work is collaborative in that we have developed the content over years of work together and it is not necessarily true that the one who speaks the most, contributes the most. Because it is the way we work together, we have kept our voices separate and in first person. You will find Russ' voice preceded by "Russ writes ..." and in a different text style.

Chapter 1: Hero Syndrome

Last weekend hundreds, perhaps thousands, of IT project team members worked unscheduled hours. Nobody considered this unusual. It happens all the time. Monday morning status reports included no mention of the unscheduled work. Some teams worked unusually hard — a heroic effort — to achieve success. These received a special mention. Others simply worked unscheduled hours. Next weekend it will happen all over again.

Since IT project heroes do not have superhuman powers — at least the ones I have met — the easiest way to be a hero is to work more hours. Heroes may do many things to differentiate themselves from unremarkable team members, but for the most part IT heroes come in early, leave late, and work over the weekend.

Why? Are we simply unwilling to pay the real cost of IT systems? Are heroic deeds really what it takes to make an IT project successful? If a successful project is based on the formula:

Predicted Effort + Unplanned Heroic Effort = Project Success

... then,

Real Project Cost = Predicted Effort + Unplanned Heroic Effort

... therefore,

Real Project Cost = Project Success

If this is true, calculating the real project cost in advance is possible and we could eliminate unplanned heroism. Since heroism remains part of many IT projects, there must be another explanation. I believe it works like this: someone made an error and now someone has to pay for that error (usually not the same someone). Heroism is then a counterbalance for error. The only way to eliminate unplanned heroism is to eliminate unplanned error. Heroism can overcome a considerable quantity of stupidity and bad judgment, but the problem is: every hero has his limits. What if you could plan the errors out of a project instead of planning heroism into it?

Unmasking a Project Hero

Mike was a project hero. He had nearly single-handedly developed the first version of a system that promised to be a big commercial success. His user interface was what the customer saw every time they used the system that promised to be a big commercial success. His user interface was what the customers saw every time they used the system and he worked harder than anyone else on the team. I was a consultant to Mike's company helping with application architecture and team organization, and developing the scale necessary to take the start-up company's product to thousands of customers.

On Tuesday, I got a call that they were going to need some software development help, something my team had not provided on this project before. I said I could be there in two or three days and we could start working on the specification then. Their response was that Mike would not last that long. Curious, I rearranged my schedule and arrived the following morning.

I met Mike on his way out. He looked horrible. The team explained: A part of the system that was supposed to transfer data between customers was not working properly and, in addition to working full days, Mike had been coming in each night to move the data manually until he could develop a solution. Nobody knew this was happening until they added several new customers with a large transaction volume and found Mike still there at 8:00 a.m.

frantically trying to get the customer's systems up and running before they finished their coffee and started work.

Over a period of several weeks, use of the system increased and Mike could no longer handle the workload. While his heroism was saving the company from embarrassment with several key early adopters, working in crisis-mode was killing him and he no longer could work on developing a solution to the problem.

Every hero has his limits. Even Superman cannot be in two places at once. Fortunately for Mike, we designed and implemented a solution before he collapsed and he was sent on mandatory vacation to recover.

As a general rule, we all like heroes. IT project heroes are usually helpful, dedicated people, the kind of people we want on our projects. We prefer stories of courage and heroism to those of a mundane life of the expected. So it is only natural that we would celebrate and congratulate the heroes around us. It is time, however, to reexamine our definition of project heroism. Given that so few of our projects are ever plagued by alien invasion, natural disaster, or a criminal mastermind, we should have very little need of heroism. Yet, in project after project, heroic efforts are required and often are not enough. Why?

Examining the Numbers

Current literature abounds with surveys and articles touting the high failure rate of IT projects. In 2004 the Standish Group's annual CHAOS report[1] showed a 100-percent improvement in software project success over 10 years achieving a mere 34-percent success rate. By 2014, another 100-percent improvement will get us only a bit ahead of throwing away every second investment. This book was written in 2008 and while I would hope for improvement in the last four years ahead of the Standish Group's curve, I don't see any evidence of it. What's worse, the Standish Group estimates these

[1] "2004 CHAOS Report." The Standish Group. Boston: Standish Group International, 2004, <www.standishgroup.com>

failures cost our industry 80 billion dollars annually despite the efforts of many project heroes. Most of these losses are cleverly hidden as baseline IT operating costs so our shareholders or partners are none the wiser. But just because we absorb them doesn't mean these losses aren't real.

Most losses are cleverly hidden as baseline IT operating costs so our shareholders or partners are none the wiser. But just because we absorb them doesn't mean these losses aren't real.

It's always dangerous to predict the future, but I suspect that if you are picking up this book in 2018, things are not so different. IT investments are likely still failing at an alarming rate and all of those losses are probably neatly hidden away in the company's books and considered simply a cost of doing business. You might think that this book should have had an impact, but as a realist and pragmatist, I find that the kind of common wisdom found herein is not commonly applied.

Before you stop reading to search for a tool with better prospects, I would also like to predict that a few organizations will have overcome the obstacles described in the pages that follow and will be getting much more from their IT investments. Unfortunately, both then and now, these companies are hard to find. If you pull up the 10K reports of U.S. public companies in a given segment, say publishing or consumer packaged goods, you will find very similar IT spending. What you don't see is any indication of IT return on investment. That is hidden in overall company performance.

If you were to isolate the IT budget for your company and combine it with the measurable increase (or decrease) in company performance that can be tied to IT investments, would your IT department look like a profit center or a large sinkhole? Granted, much of your IT budget may be fixed costs for maintaining the "plant" or corporate facilities. Just for this exercise, assume that these costs are part of the total company return. Eliminating maintenance and support of the core infrastructure, what remains should be any IT investments or project work that can be tied to some improved capability or reduced operating costs. With investment dollars going out and business benefit in dollars coming in, what is the profitability of your IT group?

Let's create an imaginary scenario. Company X is a $100 million manufacturing concern. It spends 4 percent of revenues on IT or $4 million. Let us assume that $1 million of that keeps the computers on and the network running. The remaining $3 million is investment in projects that should result in some acceptable rate of return. For the sake of convenience, we'll say 15 percent. So a $3 million investment should return $3.45 million. If 50 percent of that investment actually produces a return, then the $3 million investment produces $1.725 million or a loss of $1.275 million (42 percent). What if only 10 percent of the projects fail? Then the $3 million would produce $3.105 million or about a 0.35-percent total return. At this rate, Company X is making $1.38 million more capital available next year than a similar competitor that is only getting 50-percent success. This means you could increase your IT budget to $5.38 million next year without creating any competitive disadvantage for your firm. Not that the board would ever let you pick up a 35-percent increase to your budget, but it makes for some interesting mental gymnastics.

While I'm working the numbers, let's look at another aspect of the benefit of project success. If you need to get $3.45 million from your $3 million investment, and 50 percent of your projects fail, then the hurdle rate for any project needs to be 130 percent, to ensure that the 50 percent that succeed make up for the losses of the rest. If, however, only 10 percent of your projects fail, your hurdle rate is approximately 28 percent to achieve the same results. This means that you can take on projects with a smaller business value than your competitor who can only fund huge home-run projects.

The point to this numbers game is that discipline applied to IT investments could yield exceptional results given the state of most investments today. So why haven't reports like those from the

Standish Group spurred companies into action? To be honest they have; however, action does not equal results. Our natural inclination is to do more to get better results. If I am using 10 people to get 50-percent results, I can increase the results with 20 people. If I have a $20,000 project management tool, I can get more with a $40,000 project management tool. We spend and spend and spend and we do and do and do yet still fall prey to the non-technical problems that cause so much of our failure in the first place.

Because we often ignore hero syndrome, executives who are otherwise competent to make multi-million dollar investments through acquisitions, expansion projects, or product innovation fail to deliver on IT projects on a consistent basis. Part of the problem is they don't treat IT investments like other investments.

Mike's story is a perfect example. I call this hero syndrome. We want a silver bullet. We want a miracle. We want a hero. A part of us is skeptical every time a salesman or consultant says their tool or method offers a 30-precent productivity improvement, but somehow we hold out hope that this one really will deliver on the promise. After all, they come armed with statistics and customer references. It should be a safe bet. The problem is that those improvements come only to IT teams that are already disciplined enough to avoid the non-technical reasons for project failure. As I mentioned in the introduction, sometimes even well-disciplined project teams succumb to hero syndrome.

Because we often ignore hero syndrome, executives who are otherwise competent to make multi-million dollar investments through acquisitions, expansion projects, or product innovation fail to deliver on IT projects on a consistent basis. Part of the problem is they don't treat IT investments like other investments. I have seen, from the inside of many of America's largest companies, executives close their eyes to the apparent complexity of IT investments and simply hope for the best (a problem we specifically address later). These executives are not demanding performance, measuring returns, or assessing risks. As a result, consultants and IT staff are walking away with their money and leaving nothing to show for it.

In the introduction, I said we would place the responsibility on the executive ranks, but IT managers and developers — everyone on any failed project team — are accessories to the crime. The entire team lets this happen on project after project. You might change the tools and fire the vendors but, if you don't change how you approach and execute IT projects, don't expect different results. As one of my favorite poets says, "Meet the new boss, same as the old boss." If you want to break the cycle, you have to stop behaving like the old boss. You have to break out of the hero syndrome.

Incentivizing Failure

One problem is that our incentive systems encourage hero syndrome. This is often the same with other non-technology issues. For example, I was working on a project that required several weeks of fairly intense work. The project plan was sound and overall project risk management had been done — although not in the way Russ and I recommend. Nonetheless, the project plan was adjusted to account for anticipated risks and several items had been added to mitigate suspected problems in advance.

The team had sufficient time, expertise, and resources to get the job done on time and work hard, but not overly hard. On this project it was important that the team be alert and at their best on the final days of the project as critical thinking about a complex problem would be required at the very close of the project. Its success depended on top minds being fully engaged until the final report was made.

My role on the project was as an advisor. I would be called on to fit the results into a larger scheme, so I had a stake in the project's success. Thus, I was actively engaged with the project leaders and sometimes worked with individual teams or members as they wrestled with a tricky problem or designed a specific solution. During an early phase of the work, I spent some time observing how the team was operating and passing along my observations and recommendations to the team leads.

On one particularly frustrating day, several small things occurred that could have been prevented or easily mitigated with a simple risk plan. I showed one of the leaders how such a plan worked (you'll find it in chapter 8) and suggested that if she did a complete review weekly and a small check each day, the team could save several hours of frustration each day during this phase, and possibly in later phases. Since they were working anywhere from one to four hours extra a day, this team-level risk management would allow them to go home on time most days.

The advice fell on deaf ears. It was early enough in the project that team members weren't yet exhausted and there were many incentives to maintain the status quo. First, many of the team members were consultants or contractors who were paid by the hour. Given the importance of the project, extra hours were anticipated and budgeted. Thus, those individuals could work extra hours during this relatively short period and pocket a nice bonus from the additional hours.

The problem is the pattern of behavior. The project manager was not teaching the team leads how to manage risk within their own scope. Thus, when they became project managers, they did not know how to manage risk and failed repeatedly.

Second, both the in-house and contracted team members were sure to benefit from physically sacrificing in order to be successful. Contractors who worked hard could count on an offer to join the company — and it was a particularly desirable company. Those already on the inside could expect this effort to make a very good mark on their review, which would affect bonuses and promotions. In addition, word of mouth would make them sought after for the best projects, leading to even larger bonuses and quicker promotion. The personal incentives were particularly strong.

Third, I had no incentives to force the issue. As long as the team was poised for overall success, the day-to-day operation really was not my concern. Once the issue crossed a line where it showed up on my risk matrix, I could and would take action. Until that happened, the team members were welcome to work extra hours and reap the benefits even if I considered it a "worst practice." Since I could offer no incentives of my own — I was equipped with a stick but no carrot — I would only interfere when the issue became critical. In addition, the project plan already anticipated some necessary extra effort and several breaks were built into the schedule to keep the key thinkers fresh. All I had to do was note that the team was working particularly hard, and the project manager would ensure that the next break was not compromised. Thus the necessary controls were in place to ensure success.

Given these facts, it was natural that the project leader just nodded and then ignored my suggestions. While in all things, actual incentives like money, time, power and acknowledgement prevail, this company had a very strong "good citizen" culture and was fairly strict when it came to matters of ethics. Had this team leader taken my advice, recognized unmanaged risk, and then not acted it would have been a serious breech of ethics. On the other hand, had she taken my advice, managed the risks, and set up a structure where the team could work a normal day, she would have undermined the real incentives and affected the loyalty of her team. Ether way, the right decision was to ignore my suggestion and avoid both negative outcomes.

Thus, she learned something about risk management, but was unable to put it into practice and was rewarded for her intentional lack of discipline. The team continued to have minor issues and be frustrated with long hours and unnecessary work, but the incentives balanced against the frustration and the team maintained a healthy morale despite the inefficiency.

This team could operate in hero mode with confidence because the overall project manager was a natural risk manager and had a good track record. As a result, his resource requirements were usually approved, giving him sufficient slack to compensate for poor discipline. He could have produced equal or better results in less time or with less budget. But, compared to the rest of the organization he was a winner, so nobody noticed.

The problem is not this one instance. The problem is the pattern of behavior. The project manager was not teaching the team leads how to manage risk within their own scope. Thus, when they became project managers, they did not know how to manage risk and failed repeatedly. Consultants and internal team members were compensated for bad behavior, which they repeated on projects that were not as well managed, forcing them over budget and removing necessary slack that would be needed later. Another generation of IT "professionals" would carry hero syndrome to their projects.

Incentivizing Success

You might wonder what could be done to remedy this situation. Given only the players mentioned in my story, nothing could be done. However, there were other players not mentioned. Yes, the executives also approved the project and were watching its progress. They had neither the time nor the experience to observe what I observed, but if they were thinking about basic human behavior and the serious risk of IT project failure, they could have changed the rules.

Rule 1: Always reward success.

Every IT investment project, large or small, should carry with it a project bonus in whatever form is a sufficient motivator (e.g., money, promotion, power, cool acrylic paperweights, days off, etc.). This incentive should be based on meeting or beating three objectives: the time-line, the level of planned investment, and the level of business benefit. (See chapter 7 for more details on measurements and incentives.) If you use the right incentives and balance them with the risk and effort of the project, your best people will flock to the hardest work, which is what you want, after all.

Rule 2: Always reward discipline.

One of the reasons you don't have consistent project success is you don't have discipline. When I have the power to do so, I improve the project bonus with these objectives: The team must 1) deliver the objectives in Rule 1, AND 2) they must do so working bankers hours, producing all of the required governance components (chapter 10), and meeting or exceeding quality standards. Teams that do this get a substantial kicker to the project bonus. This will increase the status of your project management office significantly because their help in developing and maintaining discipline could mean the difference between an OK incentive and a really great one.

Rule 3: Always reward improvement.

If the project meets the objectives in Rule 1 — even if they don't meet those in Rule 2 — develop a reward sharing plan based on how much they beat the objectives in Rule 1. If the project comes in under budget, split the difference with the project team. If the project takes fewer resources, split the savings with the project team. If the project delivers a greater measurable benefit than projected, give some part of that additional benefit to the project team. Naturally, this leaves room for some gaming.

The project budget could be considerably more than needed, timelines stretched, and benefits minimized. However, this problem you can solve later. If the project cost/benefit or risk/reward is sufficient to fund it in the first place, a little gaming isn't going to hurt. If you are approving bad investments, you have a fundamentally different problem and I suggest you enroll in a MBA strategic finance course. Until you are achieving a 90-percent project success rate, don't worry about overpaying a project team or two along the way.

I'll give you an example from my own experience. Several years ago, and by that I really mean several, several years ago, I ran a consulting company that did primarily fixed-price custom software projects. We were small, fewer than 25 people, and highly specialized. For those of you who are or have been in the custom software business and don't believe you can do fixed-price development, you are the reason my company was so profitable and never lacked sufficient contracts to keep busy. While I was running the firm, we did somewhere along the lines of 35 fixed-price projects ranging from $10,000 to $500,000 and never lost money.

To keep prices to the customer low and margins high, I used two basic techniques. The first was to pay attention to the issues and follow the guidelines outlined in the following chapters. The second was to offer excellent incentives for meeting, and especially beating, estimates. I had one developer who was particularly talented. A typical work assignment for him would be between one and two weeks of effort. He worked from fixed specifications and always delivered the highest quality work. The project manager would send him the specifications for a new project and the conversation would go something like this:

Project Manager (PM): "Bill, how long will this work take you?"
Bill: "Two weeks."
PM: "You said that last time and it only took three days."
Bill: "Ok, six days."
PM: "Deal. When will I hear from you?"
Bill: "Monday."

This conversation took place on a Friday. Bill would work all weekend, often without sleep, and deliver the finished work product on Monday. He would then proceed to take the rest of the week off. Had I asked him to come to work every day from 8:00 a.m. to 5:00 p.m., the work would have taken him six days. But, because he was motivated by having control over his own time, I got the finished product days early and could tackle other parts of the system that would have waited for his component.

Granted, this kind of interaction requires some experience with and trust in your individual team members. But even as we added new team members, it only took a few assignments to determine if their time estimates were reasonable. We would start a new team member on a assignment for which we had a good internal benchmark and compare both their estimate and actual productivity against it. Generally, if team members were overestimating, we negotiated them down, but in Bill's case, he gave reasonable estimates for a typical work week and then worked like crazy to buy himself some free time.

I never asked Bill to work on the time he had earned for himself, but I always had a few really interesting side projects in the queue. If he got bored — which often happened — he would pick up something fun, but not urgent, and work on it for free. I had agreed to pay for six days of work for the component he delivered and, as a result of the incentive system, he was rewarded. Because of some knowledge of basic human nature, I always got more than I paid for and all my people were extremely happy.

An important point to note is that I did not spend more money than my budget allowed for full-time resources. Compensation does not always have to come in the form of more money, and you can usually find a way to work around any corporate limitations in that regard. Then again, sometimes incentives are all about the money.

Effective Incentives

You must be sure your incentives are effective and not believe that your people are properly motivated simply because you have created what you perceive to be an incentive.

You must be sure your incentives are effective and not believe that your people are properly motivated simply because you have created what you perceive to be an incentive. I have found, for example, that the acrylic project trophies so common in corporations today motivate only a very small number of people. These people are easy to identify because their desks are littered with these oversized paperweights. Remember that only some of your people will work harder or have better focus because a trophy waits them at the end of the task. Save some project money and give these rewards only to the people who care about them. Everyone else will need something different. Each group and each individual will require a different set of incentives. One of my favorite T-shirt quotes is, "The floggings will continue until morale improves." (Not that I recommend flogging as a motivator.) Be creative and develop incentives that will work for your IT group or project team, fit within the budget and rules, and begin to eliminate hero syndrome.

We're going to talk more about heroism as it affects your IT projects in chapter 13 including the dark side of heroism — something you may personally have to resist. Take away from this chapter the fact that hero syndrome is alive and well on your projects. If not specifically institutionalized heroism, then one or more of the other items on our top-ten list plagues your projects time after time. Your job is to recognize the danger and develop a plan to remove hero syndrome from your IT investments.

Chapter 2:
Our Tools

Selecting Tools

L et me warn you up front, very little in this book is original. The old tricks are the best tricks and we have endevoured to put the best tricks to work to improve the chances of project success. We practice techniques invented by myriad experts who have done research and have practical experience in systems architecture, business organization, analysis, design, anthroplolgy and other fields. These pioneers have developed many tools, but not every tool has stood the test of practical application. Our work has been to try these tools out on real projects. We have — over the span of more than twenty years — sifted through both popular and lesser-known literature searching for ways to prevent or better manage both technical and non-technical issues on our projects. We tried to apply anything that looked promising. Techniques that moved us toward greater success we retained, others we modified and tried again, and the impractical we left behind.

To combat hero syndrome and improve your rate of IT project success, we will introduce a variety of tools, techniques, and processes that we believe are effective in managing non-technical issues in many situations. I can't promise you that everything we talk about will fit your situation or that every tool will produce excellent results. However, both Russ and I promise that we have used all of our recommendations in real projects and that they have helped us achieve greater success. We have selected our issues and our tools based on a set of simple rules. I'll talk more about the issues later, but our tools always follow these rules:

Rule 1: Easy to use

If a tool takes more than a few minutes or a few pages of explanation, it is too complicated. Reducing complexity is a key part of successfully managing issues. Understanding your business, the language of your industry, your organization and internal power structures, the proposed value of the project, and the solution options is difficult enough. Adding complexity in your management tools is unnecessary. This doesn't mean that mastery of a tool or technique is immediate. Learning to roll a bowling ball takes mere minutes, but mastering the technique is considerably more difficult. Nevertheless, any tool needs to be easy enough to be useful immediately and, where mastery takes time, the value of the tool should improve with time. This leads us to Rule 2.

Rule 2: Valuable

The tool or technique should provide more value than the effort required. Generally this means significantly more value; however, as I explained in Rule 1, a tool may provide some value immediately and more as you master it. Tools that require too much effort will not be used; but, just because a tool is easy to use does not mean it is useful. Never spend your valuable time with the valueless.

Rule 3: Easy to explain

Related to easy to use, this rule says you must be able to quickly and simply tell others what you are doing. Diagrams, charts, process steps, and structures all may help you manage tough issues, but if your project team or sponsors don't understand what it all means and how it brings value, they are as likely to work at cross-purposes with you as they are to support the effort. My rule of thumb is that you have three to five minutes to explain a tool (err on the short side) before you lose the attention of your audience.

However, once a powerful and effective tool is understood, you will find it drift into other projects and other parts of the organization. I have several times been thrilled to see one of the tools that Russ and I use appear in a completely unexpected place.

Rule 4: Pencil and paper

I cut my teeth on software and systems architecture during the heyday of computer automated software engineering, or CASE tools. These tools — usually $50,000 to $100,000 a seat — were complex pieces of engineering that purported to automate what were, at the time, the most popular diagrams depicting logical and physical views of IT systems. CASE tools broke Rules 1, 2, and 3. Nevertheless, I dived into this new area with gusto. As a systems architect, I was sure that our "systems" issues could and should be managed with a system. The effective demise of the industry shows how wrong I was.

As I learned, like many others, that the tools were too complex and required too many specialized resources, I continually drifted back to the white board and the restaurant napkin. I have found that the best tools can be used everywhere and must be available for use anywhere. Important decisions are made on golf courses, in hotel bars, and in hallways where overhead projectors and high-powered workstations are not available. Pencil and paper are almost universally available and I have even resorted to scratching diagrams in the dirt on the sidelines of a sporting event. Those dirt drawings were more effective than any I developed with a CASE tool.

Rule 5: Low-fidelity

Anything you do must be open to criticism. The best tools require collaboration, review, and critique.

Anything you do must be open to criticism. The best tools require collaboration, review, and critique.

Diversity of perspective is a popular trend, and our experience has born out that such diversity is essential to getting the most out of these tools and techniques. When you develop a communications plan, a risk matrix, or a context diagram (explained in later chapters) using a fancy graphics or presentation tool, your work appears complete. You make a presentation and everyone smiles and nods. Nobody wants to embarrass you or themselves by suggesting that you missed something important or that you have made an incorrect assumption. OK, maybe "nobody" is too broad a group. People like me enjoy a good fight and don't hesitate to criticize everything — but that is why I don't get invited to these presentations very often.

If, instead of a polished presentation, you represent your "straw man" idea in a way that literally looks like it was made from straw, your peers consider it a draft. You can't have spent much time on it — even if it took days to develop. They are then much more open to making observations or providing guidance. Even after getting good feedback, I encourage you to keep things looking unfinished. This allows you to iterate, as I explain in the next rule.

Rule 6: Iterative

Conditions change, time passes, people move on, and priorities shift. All these require you to reevaluate many aspects of a project. Iteration is essential to any good tool. If your tools don't let you easily try again, or modify or adapt your work, you will find that they are more a cause of project failure than the issue you were using the tool to resolve in the first place. You may use a strongly iterative IT methodology or one that is more linear; however, the tools used to attack our top-ten issues must be open to change. At regular intervals or critical stage-gates, you must ensure that you are still on track and an issue has not crept back into your project.

Rule 7: Focus on flaws

It is theoretically impossible to prove that any complex system is perfect — especially where humans are involved. So stop trying. Instead, use tools that help lead you quickly to errors and flaws. The absence of obvious flaws does not necessarily mean you have removed them all, but if you can quickly zero in on the most important ones, you greatly increase your chances of success.

When I speak to software developers, I ask them if they intentionally create errors in their software. They universally respond that they do not. I then ask them if they have ever created a complex piece of software that had no errors the first time. The general consensus is that they have not. Despite this fact, they hold out hope in every new project that this time they will build the right thing the first time. I don't want to be the cause of widespread depression among software developers, but a little pragmatic reality is needed. If you always make mistakes, then stop believing you won't. You are going to be wrong. Given that fact, find tools that help you find those flaws as quickly as possible so you can overcome errors early and move on to more interesting and productive work.

Russ writes: Adopting this rule personally had a more profound affect on the way I approach many parts of my work than I would've believed, and it took me quite some time to realize just how powerful it was.

Looking back to my early days as an application developer, I can recall many times where, in presenting anything from a design concept to a nearly finished application, I was eagerly trying to convince my customer that the design was the right solution, or that the application was functioning properly. While there may be times when there is value in this kind of exercise, what I didn't realize was how much feedback it was preventing my customers from giving me, especially those who were quiet, shy, or not inclined to disagree with me.

As I gained expertise and seniority, this problem became worse. People were less inclined to question me because they considered me an "expert," while they were not. It was exactly this issue between a very senior pilot and a junior flight engineer that contributed to two Boeing 747s colliding, resulting in one of the worst accidents in aviation history[2].

---

[2] "Tenerife Disaster." Wikipedia: The Free Encyclopedia. 8 November 2008 <en.wikipedia.org/wiki/Tenerife_disaster#Chain_of_events_leading_to_disaster>

Now that I've shifted to taking an "assume it's wrong" approach, I get much better feedback, which is usually what I need most. When it comes time to review, I generally start the conversation with a statement like, "This (document, entry screen, report) isn't done yet and I'm sure I've gotten it wrong somewhere. Can you help me figure out where the mistakes are?" Now, instead of challenging, even daring people to tell me I'm wrong ("I hate to tell you this Russ, but I think there may be a problem"), instead they can tell me I'm wrong by agreeing with me ("Yeah you're right Russ, your solution is totally screwed up!")

This concept will definitely rub some readers the wrong way. "The last thing I'm going to do is encourage people to blow holes in something I just spent the last six months working on!" This is why the next rule (i.e., front-load risks) is so important.

Rule 8: Front-load risks

The concept of front-loading risks is quite simple: The sooner you find out something is going to go wrong, the more time you will have to make it right, and the less work you might have to throw away.

The concept of front-loading risks is quite simple: The sooner you find out something is going to go wrong, the more time you will have to make it right, and the less work you might have to throw away. The tools we select help us bring the toughest, or hardest to manage, problems to the forefront.

Russ writes: *Time is the most valuable asset in any project, as it is the most finite resource. Although you could argue that you can often extend deadlines, the fact that there are 60 minutes to an hour and 24 hours to a day is absolutely inescapable. No amount of manpower or money can change that. The example I often use when presenting our workshop is actually about preparing to for the workshop itself.*

Since we typically fly somewhere to present our workshop, the night before I always check to make sure I have shirt, pants, shoes, and belt accounted for and ready to go. Although it may appear a little obsessive (OK, maybe it is a little obsessive!), I'm actually front-loading the risk of not having the right clothes for the workshop. If I waited until the morning of the workshop, only to discover that I forgot my belt, what are my options at that point, besides paper-clipping my pants to my shirt? However, if I check the night before and discover my mistake, I have plenty of time to buy a new one.

Rule 9: Self-testing

This rule assumes that anything you do is testable. If you cannot determine that you had a positive effect, then stop doing what you are doing. All your tools must lead you to measurable results. Additionally, the best tools are their own test. Such tools expose flaws as a natural part of using them, or have checks and balances built into their process of use. One step should confirm another, or one part should expose the flaws in another.

Rule 10: Self-leveling

Leveling is a more technical aspect to project tools. Traditionally, the term leveling has been used in software engineering to describe a process to make sure that items on one technical diagram are represented by their appropriate counterparts on another, or that all items at an abstract viewpoint are represented in more detailed views of the same information. We mean something similar here, but perhaps a little less technical. One of the tools I always use on a project is called the business purpose (chapter 5). In this short document, you must describe the who, what, when, where, why, and how of a project. If you later make a training plan for your project, you will describe at least who (who gets trained and who trains them), how (classroom, in the field, on-line), and when.

If any who, how, or when in your training plan does not fit with your business purpose, one of the two documents is wrong. Getting them right is what I call leveling. For your training plan to be a tool that follows Rule 10, it must encourage you to use, check, or otherwise integrate with other tools — such as the business purpose — such that when you have a completed training plan it is already leveled with other tools.

Rule 11: Self-documenting

If there's one thing I hate, it is to have developed an elegant design, or established a promising process only to spend the next several weeks documenting it all. The tools that allow you to think creatively and manage risks effectively should be their own documentation. You should never be faced with the closing question typical in many meetings, "OK, who is going to write all of this down?" Select tools that, even when low-fidelity, work as-is and don't need to be reformatted. Also give up on the notion that everything has to be pretty to be useful.

I do a considerable amount of paper or low-fidelity prototyping. (You can learn a little more about this technique in appendix A.) This is a pencil-and-paper prototype illustrating what screens will look like. These are often interesting, but rarely of art-gallery quality. Nevertheless, I have taken photocopies of these hand-drawn screens together with hand written notes and diagrams, put them together in a binder and presented it as the system specification to executives for approval. A few times, I have had to explain why the team did not waste any time making these documents pretty. But, I do not usually receive any negative comments and in all cases the documents have been sufficient basis for investment decision making.

Testing your tools

This probably seems like an overly long list of rules. The good news is you only need to apply them if you are adding tools to your toolkit. We can assure you the tools we discuss in this book already pass the test. You are welcome to check our work, by evaluating anything we suggest against these rules. So far, we have given you two tools. The first was in chapter 1: the three rules of developing incentives for your project team. How does it fair against these ten rules?

It is easy to use (Rule 1). You can check your current incentive plan in just a few minutes and can develop ideas for an alternative through a quick brainstorming session. Checking your ideas is a simple exercise of evaluating it against the rules in order one to three. It is valuable (Rule 2). Hopefully the example I provided showed that value, but there's nothing like trying it yourself to see if it is. Although, with practice, you will get better at developing effective incentive systems, you should get some value from the tool immediately by simply checking what you do now.

It is easy to explain (Rule 3). I took only a few pages to lay out the rules and provide an example. It is a pencil-and-paper exercise (Rule 4). You will have to put any resulting incentive scheme into a human-resources system or some formal documentation; however, this requires only a few checkmarks on the back of a napkin. It is certainly low-fidelity (Rule 5) or can be depending on how you present your results and recommendations. You can iterate (Rule 6) as often as you wish without difficulty. It is completely focused on finding flawed incentive plans (Rule 7) and it is itself a test so it fits the self-testing rule (Rule 8).

You can front-load the risks of the plan by playing a simple "what-if" exercise with your team — "What if we put this incentive plan into place?" (Rule 9) Exposing failures in a current or proposed incentive plan will lead you to other issues. Thus, it is at least somewhat self-leveling (Rule 10). The documentation is simply a description of the incentives and a statement that your incentive plan meets one or more of the rules; easy if not actually self-documenting (Rule 11).

The rule of "good enough"

I have one more rule that applies throughout this book. It is the rule of "good enough" systems. Perhaps you work in a field where perfect is the only acceptable answer, say manned space flight or critical health care. Or you may work in an organization that practices six-sigma regularly. In those cases, you are working closer and closer to perfection and have a very low tolerance for error. I can assure you that, in the case of managing the non-technical causes of project failure, perfection is not necessary. In most systems, computer, human or otherwise, good enough is, well, good enough.

> *An unhealthy search for perfection is also a sign of hero syndrome.*

An unhealthy search for perfection is also a sign of hero syndrome. If no method is good enough for your organization or for a specific individual, beware. We IT professionals have a tendency to be detailed-oriented and the kind of work we do requires precision (i.e., the blue cable goes in the left socket and the red cable goes in the right socket).

We take our methods and tools very seriously. Frequently, this goes to the level or religious battles over techniques, products, and perspectives. When perfection is confused with precision, you will find your team working over a weekend because "the emerging IEEE standard for cable coloring states that orange is the correct color for left-socket connections" and they are replacing all of the blue cables with orange ones. Such work demands heroes who will work without rest to bring your infrastructure up to modern standards. You may want to introduce those heroes to the concept of "good enough."

You will find the tools we recommend and the techniques we espouse don't follow the ten rules perfectly. Even the example I gave was weak in a few areas. Nonetheless, it provides good enough value and the search for a more perfect tool is just not worth the effort. This thinking pervades not only our selection of tools but how we use them. You don't need to develop the absolutely perfect incentive system; you just need to have a better one to get some value. By combining good enough now with iteration, you can improve over time.

Chapter 3:
Our Top-Ten Issues

"All the really important mistakes are made the first day."

— *The Art of Systems Architecting*[3]

Several years ago, Russ and I were consultants together at the same company. We visited a new client to implement some new methods for rapidly deriving system requirements. Our CEO joined us on the visit. He was there to see these methods in practice to determine if we could teach them to the rest of the consulting group, and he was anxious to establish a long-term relationship with the client. Our firm was small and this client was well respected and would help open doors in a critical market segment. It was important to us to do both excellent work and the right work. Our understanding of the importance of the latter probably saved us from foolishness.

We spent several hours that morning drawing diagrams and developing an understanding of the business problem the client faced. As we worked with the project stakeholders, it became obvious to both Russ and me that an off-the-shelf product could easily solve this client's problem. We could probably halt the analysis, direct them to the appropriate product, and allow the client team to continue without further help from our firm. I called for a short break.

---

[3] Maier, Mark W. and Eberhardt Rechtin. The Art of Systems Architecting. Second Edition. Boca Raton, Florida: CRC Press, 2000.

The consulting team discussed the situation during the break. We could continue with the analysis and develop a custom solution, thereby increasing our revenues and developing an area of expertise almost certain to drive additional business. On the other hand, we could tell the customer that a reasonable commercial product already existed and could be installed quickly and easily.

The client had hired us for our expertise and our understanding of the market. They didn't want us to create a situation where a hero would be required.

The second option would be cheapest for the customer, but would not do much to accomplish our business goals. Fortunately for this customer, we clearly understood the difference between "expert" and "hero." The client had hired us for our expertise and our understanding of the market. They didn't want us to create a situation where a hero would be required. We called a close to the analysis and helped them install a trouble-free, off-the-shelf solution.

This may sound more like a business ethics challenge than a close call with hero syndrome. But I have found that hero syndrome is just as likely to cause a failure in ethics as is a desire for financial gain. To be an IT hero, you have to do something heroic, which means you have to develop or encourage a crisis requiring heroism. In this example, our struggle was against the desire to build something better, something more closely aligned with the business problem. This "better" system would naturally require the continued attention of the experts who built it and occasionally would require them to swoop in as heroes to save the day when something we built didn't really work the way it was supposed to.

The twisted logic that accompanies hero syndrome is so common it is rarely even noticed. Yet, it is exactly that kind of thinking that brings so many IT projects to their ruin. Our aim is to expose this wrong-headed approach and give you a fresh perspective on how your projects are doing. Focusing on the hero syndrome, Russ and I have collaborated to bring you our combined top-ten list of non-technical causes of project failure. These are the issues we find most prevalent and most dangerous.

Selecting Issues

As you saw in the previous chapter, Russ and I use a fair amount of rigor in selecting and testing our tools. Even when we are satisfied with good enough, we don't settle for just anything. We follow the research and literature. We test promising tools against a set of well understood rules. We try the technique in practice. You could say we have a methodology. It is then natural to be curious about the science behind how we selected the top-ten list of issues. That is an excellent question. I'm glad you asked. Are there any other questions? No? Then we will move on to our next topic.

Of course I'm avoiding the answer. Frankly, there's no science. We didn't conduct a survey, spend government money on a study, or hire a bunch of graduate students to sift through piles of data. Instead, we relied on our experience working on IT (and non-IT) projects over the past 20-plus years.

So when we first decided to speak on this topic, we sat down together in a hotel lobby bar with a napkin and pencil — actually it might have been one of those hotel mini-notepads and a pen with the hotel logo on it — and we started brainstorming. We were going to stop at five, but the list kept getting longer. When we got to ten, we were pretty satisfied. We then spent some time exploring other issues not on the list to see if any of them should replace one of the original ten. As it turned out, none did. How did we, in the course of less than an hour, come to a consensus on the top-ten non-technical problems that plague IT projects? Simple: a boatload of hard-earned experience.

They say it's not bragging if you have done it, but people who talk about how good they are still get on my nerves (even when I'm the one doing it). Nevertheless, I'll give you an idea of where we have been in the last twenty years. Individually or together we have:

- Run a U.S. Army intelligence center during wartime
- Negotiated IT contracts in Asia because the woman running the facility was … well … a woman in an Asia run by men (don't even get me started)
- Redesigned the infrastructure of a medical equipment manufacturer so that an email the CIO sent to himself would arrive in less than the 30 minutes it was taking.
- Designed an application to manage detailed data on all of the cellular providers in Latin America (back when there were even more than there are today)
- Wrote a few lines of software to replace a twenty-year-old system that had held a major insurance company hostage because nobody understood what it did
- Translated cryptic symbolic software that determined chemical formulas for a glue manufacturer into a modern and user-maintainable system
- Helped a foreign aid agency process resumes so they could place experts on the right projects
- Helped a major cable content provider move its operations from Hong Kong to Singapore
- Helped a company move its data center from the city to the suburbs
- Developed a process and application to facilitate the movement of engineering documents between a U.S. high-tech manufacturer and an Asian partner
- Transformed a government agency incapable of meeting information processing objectives into a high-performing organization that regularly exceeded expectations (yes, sometimes public institutions can be efficient)
- Helped a promising executive get a promotion by enabling his department to better handle their workload

… and the list goes on.

It is one thing to offer advice based on a string of successes that could very well have been a result of heroism and quite another to have had a sufficient number of failures to understand what made the difference. I have never liked the books that promised me I could get rich, invest wisely, become influential, negotiate like a pro, or some other thing when they were written by a guy or gal who had this one success and had never fallen flat on their face (or choose another part of the anatomy). You can be sure that Russ and I carry plenty of battle scars. I have done some pretty stupid things and sometimes done many of the right things and still achieved miserable results, for example:

- Having failed to understand key indicators, I allowed events to go unreported that caused devastating consequences to an important operation.

- Solving the wrong problem and using the wrong people, I squandered an important investment for the manager of a regional distribution center, making it impossible for him to meet his customers' needs.

- After months of analysis and considerable expense, I delivered a strategy that was completely overcome by events predictable to even a casual observer.

- Having turned a blind eye to obvious executive shortcomings, I was an active participant in the demise of an otherwise promising technology company resulting in complete loss for all investors, lawsuits and bankruptcy for the principles, and a personal financial disaster.

We learn the most from our failures. Our top-ten list comes more from that hard experience than it does from our many successes.

In addition to overall project success or failure, together we have met possibly the world's most challenging individuals and been faced with political infighting, project teams running at the ragged edge, utter stupidity, and good intentions gone horribly wrong.

These are the real conditions inside even successful projects and contributed strongly to our list.

You are more than welcome to disagree with our choices, they are our own after all. But, even if you would have some others in your top-ten list, these are sufficiently important that you ignore them at your peril. I can think of no project failure with which I have had contact where one or more of these items did not play a significant role in causing the project to fail.

Most important, these are failures of executive management. Many different players may have a hand in any of these, but executives who sponsor or approve IT projects are ultimately responsible to prevent these problems from aborting their investment. You can fire the entire IT department and hire a fresh crew and these problems will persist. You have to eradicate them, particularly at the executive level, and then continually combat them at all levels. The chapters that follow provide more detail about each problem, how they occur, what effect they have and how to deal with them. We will wrap it all up in the final chapter with some ideas on how to survive these issues and how to take your first steps toward greater IT project success.

Here's what was written on that napkin:

Issue 1: Believing the hype

Blindly accepting the statements of both your internal team and your vendors is asking for trouble. We'll explain why IT hype is so common and what to do about it.

Issue 2: Solving the wrong problem

This is manifest in two ways: Either your team has a different idea than you do about what your business does, or what they heard is not what you said. Both of these lead to solving the wrong problem. A good set of checks and balances early in the project can prevent this.

Issue 3: Using the wrong people

Sometimes the wrong people are all you have to work with. But, if you only have two masons and a carpenter, we do not recommend taking on plumbing projects.

Issue 4: Measuring the wrong things

You get what you measure, so be very careful what you measure because that's what you'll get.

Issue 5: Hope as a risk management strategy

A little risk management goes a long way. Good financial managers are laser focused on risk. Why is IT project risk management so frequently ignored?

Issue 6: Round is a shape (not keeping fit)

Your technical team got a lot of intense technical training in the beginning of their career. When was the last time your twenty-year veterans had a work out?

Issue 7: Ignorance as a defense

First-order ignorance (you don't know) is bad enough, but it is second-order ignorance (you don't know what you don't know) is what kills IT projects. We take a look at second-order ignorance and show you how to get your arms around the problem.

Issue 8: Ostrichism (ignoring complexity)

This is related to ignorance, but worse. It is the conscious effort to remain ignorant, even when you know better. You might be surprised how many times you see a problem coming at your IT project and you pretend it isn't there.

Issue 9: Giving perception sway (not communicating reality)

Poor communication is a critical cause of Issue 2, solving the wrong problem. But even when you are solving the right problem, you need to keep communicating reality. Your organization will determine the meaning of an event or decide on the status of a project on their own — accurately or not — if you do not keep them informed. Similarly, if your staff is rewarded for bearing only good news, you won't know what hit you when you find yourself under the train wreck.

Issue 10: A hero behind every tree

Hero syndrome, at its worst, is found in projects where heroism is actively planned in. All of the above issues contribute to the need for a project hero, but sometimes we maintain hero syndrome through the dark side of heroism, firefighting

Chapter 4:
Believing the Hype

In 1992, I found myself in the position of extensively evaluating the cutting-edge computer aided software engineering (CASE) tools of the day. I had recently been certified in Software Engineering by the Institute for the Certification of Computing Professionals (ICCP) and therefore felt I had some relevant expertise that qualified me to evaluate such tools. One sure sign of impending stupidity is the belief that you are a qualified expert. I had spent weeks reading books by Capers Jones and Clive Finkelstein and had attended lectures by the Three Amigos of the emerging object-oriented movement. I was a very self-confident evaluator.

The dot-com craze hadn't begun, but 1992 is when all of those dot-com CEOs were cutting their teeth. Powerful workstations were becoming affordable for specialized uses, and promising new software and tools were making personal computers and local-area-networks viable as business tools. The Internet as we know it today did not exist. The World Wide Web consisted of 26 servers, and a generally usable browser was still a year away. So, the focus of most software development was on systems used inside the four walls of a business. Battling for mindshare in this space were companies like Microsoft, Apple, Sun, and IBM along with scores of smaller companies with niche software languages, databases, or software development tools. CASE was going to tame the wild west of software development and allow us to work across many platforms, preventing any one vendor from dominating the desktop — you can see how well that worked.

While investors and the world in general had not become crazed with technology optimism — that would happen in a few years — the engineers most certainly had. I was one of those engineers. I began developing software on mainframes using engineering and end-user languages rather than the more traditional corporate COBOL. I quickly moved to personal computers and a dizzying collection of system and software language names and acronyms including CP/M, DOS, Xenix, Fortran, EXECII, Z80 Assembler, Pascal, REXX, C, Ada, Actor, Visual Basic (not like those other basics), SQL, Lisp, and several languages and tools so proprietary to various database or groupware systems that most of their names would be meaningless to even the most technical of readers. I was an eager participant in the wild west of software development, quite convinced of my skills, ready to be a hero … and the perfect target for a skilled salesman.

I evaluated all the leading CASE vendors and several that looked promising, but had yet to develop a customer base. The company for which I worked was fairly conservative, so I had to develop a strong business case for any purchase we might make. My role was to explore these kinds of technologies and determine what might make a good investment. We held review meetings and had three vendors do live trials as a sort of face-off competition. During the whole process we got hype and more hype. We saw vapor-ware, software that didn't really exist but looked good in a scripted demo — or was simply a point in someone's presentation with no reality at all behind it. We saw engineers trying desperately to install software that salesmen had demonstrated only yesterday. We saw systems being "fixed" in the field right before our eyes — so much for configuration management.

During the many months when I was under a daily deluge of hype, I attended some seminars on object-oriented analysis and design. The speaker — I cannot remember who it was — told us, as if in confidence, that the productivity claims of many new methods and tools were no longer believed by corporate management. Claims of 30-50-percent productivity improvements were not convincing arguments. His experience had shown that his methods achieved a greater than

30-percent productivity improvement, but we should tell our management that they would get a 13-percent improvement. This number was more believable as well as appearing to be more precise and was sufficient to justify the cost of consulting, training and tools. When we then delivered better than expected results we would be heroes! I was, I admit, stupid enough to think this a clever argument.

I am fairly sure the tools we finally installed are no longer used by the organization. I do not know for certain, but I would be willing to bet that very few of the practices that the CASE tools embodied are, or were ever, seriously used at my former company. Nonetheless, I sold CASE every bit has hard as the vendors did, wasting a considerable amount of my time and effort and an embarrassingly large chunk of the IT budget.

Fighting the Eternal Optimists

The problem with hype is that it comes from two sources: your vendors and your internal staff. IT people are, in general, optimists. The 1990s not withstanding, something in the makeup of systems professionals generates and even requires optimism. We are, after all, faced regularly with problems we have never solved before. Without plenty of natural optimism we would be immobilized by the sheer weight of the unknown. Unfortunately, this trait also works against us. After several successes we are sure that we can solve any problem and

The problem with hype is that it comes from two sources: your vendors and your internal staff.

construct any system and we therefore seriously underestimate the effort required. Or as in the case of my CASE tool encounter, we overestimate the value of some new system or method. You can and should consider any statement about individual or organizational IT capability to be a myth or an outright lie, regardless of the earnestness or good intent of the people delivering the message.

We IT professionals believe our own hype in this regard and are convinced of the truth of our abilities. I recently evaluated a proven and reliable software team who spoke convincingly about their capabilities with a particular new technology. They had performed well using other technologies and I needed these new skills to take on a really complex project. They assured my evaluation team they had mastered the new technology. However, when pressed, they admitted to having no formal training, having produced no relevant contributions to the industry to show mastery, and having developed only trivial systems using the technology. I liked them and they had performed well on other projects, but I simply couldn't accept the risk of trusting their assessment with regard to the effort necessary to complete the project when they had so little on which to base it. It would be the same as asking a professional guitar player to tell you how long it would take to tune a piano. It's just more strings, right?

Getting the hype from your internal IT staff is bad enough, but add a professional salesman or two to the mix and you have considerably more hype than reality. The days of CASE tools have not deterred people from developing and selling IT systems both large and small. I have worked with some really excellent salespeople. Only a very, very few can resist the urge to over promise — just a little. After all, their technical teams have performed miracles in the past. They feed the hype of their capability to the sales team as constantly as the sales team feeds it to potential customers.

Compound the problem with the fact that good salesmen are rarely also good technologists — and the two speak different languages. Sometimes a sales over-promise is due to misunderstanding rather than zeal. I can clearly remember hearing one of my salesmen telling a customer what we would deliver in their new system, some of which was to my ears completely untrue. On confronting the salesman afterwards, I found he had misunderstood our acronyms and technical terms and honestly thought he was describing in the customer's language what we had already built. As you might imagine, sorting all that out with the customer was a bit challenging. Even when with good intentions, this is the state of the systems marketplace. Any vendor who solicits your business is bringing you sales claims on top of IT claims, a dangerous combination.

Identify and Verify

How do you keep from believing the hype? When faced with a tough business issue, you want a vendor or internal staff member to swoop in with a solution. A sales cold-call for something you don't need is easy to dismiss, but when you call in your best vendors to evaluate viable, working solutions how do you sort fact from hype?

First identify the claims, and second verify them. Employ executive skills and get to the heart of the matter. What exactly are you being promised? Only the clearest of deals can be done verbally. Get those promises in writing. One of the best ways to understand fact versus hype is to write out your understanding of the promises. After any meeting where someone is trying to convince you to spend money or take action that would benefit them or their constituents, draft a simple memo describing what you understood to be the core promises and ask for a confirmation of your understanding. Simple errors will be quickly corrected. Intentional misdirection will be harder to identify, but you will have established a basis on which to throw them out of the building if you find intentional deception is part of their sales strategy.

You may trust your teams and want to believe them to be dealing with you in an open and honest manner. Honor and ethics are not dead in business and yours may be such a place. I can't judge your team or your partners through the pages of this book; however, I can tell you how to deal with me. I am a straight-shooter, which often gets me into trouble. I firmly try not to promise what I cannot deliver. Were you to do business with me, you should expect me to have both of our interests at heart and deal in the facts as much as possible.

All this being true, you should still not believe my hype. As I said earlier, we IT types are optimists. I tend much more toward pragmatism (or this book would not be possible) and some IT people consider me downright pessimistic. Nonetheless, I believe in a positive outcome and frequently fall prey to unrealistic zeal. If I say something that sounds like a promise, confirm it in writing and my more sensible side will remove any hype before I agree to what is in written form. When dealing with your team, you should approach them in a non-threatening manner or even make the communication fault your own. "I want to be sure I understand what I heard you to say…" This will prevent insult, but also protect your interests from the hype almost always present in IT promises.

Another technique I find useful, particularly in group settings is to pretend. This is a common sales technique and many of the group will be comfortable with it. Simply project the promises into a future in which they have to be delivered. You can say something like, "Let's imagine that I say yes to your proposal. In six months from today your Hoojiebop 6000 will be fully operational in my data center and my systems monitoring costs will at that point immediately be reduced by 20 percent because I can, without any other effort, disconnect my Oldgizmo 1500 and no longer pay for maintenance and support. All of my staff will already be trained on the new system and there will be no noticeable change in the operation. Is that a correct projection of the future?" The guys with the Hoojiebop will probably want to confer before the meeting proceeds.

Once you have a clear understanding of the promise, then require evidence that the team can deliver. Much of the evidence you will hear will be useless because the team is measuring the wrong thing (chapter 7) and much will be a claim based on unrelated experience. You may need to employ an advisor to help you understand what is the same and what is different with regard to specific technology. But the rule to keep in mind is, if you want your team to swim the English Channel, no amount of success on a golf course is evidence of the team's capability in the water.

Verification is about managing risk, not proving your team wrong or right. Trust your IT team and your technology partners, but always, always verify their capability.

Both Russ and I are huge fans of the Regan-era "trust but verify" concept. I don't want to say all your vendors and IT staff are liars, or intentionally creating distracting hype. They completely believe what they are saying. With few exceptions, I believe what I am saying and will stand firm that it is right ... until I change my mind. Verification is about managing risk, not proving your team wrong or right. Trust your IT team and your technology partners, but always, always verify their capability.

The toughest part of working in the technology field is that most of our investment projects have one or more unique aspects. The power, and also the danger, of software is that you can design it to new purposes. We IT people do this all the time. Therefore if you ask us if we can you do something we've never done before, the answer is of course! We have, after all, done something new on every project we have participated in over the length of our careers. Our ability to tackle the unique is common to the industry. Here's what you really want to know: Can we tackle this specific uniqueness within the constraints of the project? To reduce the risks, you want a team for whom the greatest part of your project is routine.

You can apply some basic statistics here. If your team has not done essentially the same thing you are asking now at least 30 times, then you have an inadequate sample size, so keep that in mind. If your team has not accurately recorded the delta between estimate and actual on previous projects, you have no way of measuring their accuracy and, therefore, have no way to verify claims. In the unlikely event that you have a reasonable sample size of well-tracked estimate versus actual deltas, you can develop a confidence interval to apply to your team's hype. I like to measure three things: budget, delivery dates, and promised business improvement. I have found that adding as much as 50 percent to 100 percent to budget and time estimates is not unreasonable. I have yet to encounter an organization that tracks business improvement in a way effective enough for statistical hype-busting.

So, chances are you don't have any useful measurements, or the few you do have are clearly not statistically significant. How do you manage the hype? If you have done your best to identify and confirm the promises, and made a reasonable attempt to compare the team's results on similar work, you are ahead of most of your competitors. The next steps will make the difference. You must solve the right problem (chapter 5), use the right people (chapter 6), measure the right things (chapter 7), manage your risks (chapter 8) ... I think you get the idea. Remember, even if you use simple measurements, the key to hype-busting is to trust but verify.

Our VRS Integrates with Your Purchasing System

Russ writes: I have been working with a fleet management company for several years. They maintain a large number of vehicles and other equipment, and both purchase and stock a large number of items to keep them running. One of my main responsibilities during my tenure there was to develop and maintain their purchasing and inventory control system. It is a completely custom-developed system, tailored specifically to the way they operate. I'll call it MYSYS from this point forward.

Several years ago, they decided their maintenance operation was inefficient and somewhat reactionary, and it needed to be vastly improved. They embarked on an entire business process re-engineering project, and determined that part of the overall process improvement would be to implement a new maintenance management system (called VRS) that would handle everything from vehicle maintenance scheduling, work order generation, parts requests, parts room stock, and preventative maintenance schedules. Based on the information they collected, they compiled requirements, published a request for proposal (RFP) and collected responses. After several dog-and-pony shows, one of the responders (whom I will call the Winner from here on) was awarded a contract to implement the VRS system. The solution the Winner offered my client was an existing VRS that would be customized to make it fit my client's needs.

I was largely uninvolved in the business process reengineering and

RFP/award process, although I did contribute briefly when it came time to discuss how parts and stock would be purchased, as the purchasing part of the overall process would still be handled by MYSYS, and MYSYS would need to "integrate" with the VRS to exchange information. Let's take a moment to think about that term:

Integrate (verb) – to form, coordinate or blend into a functioning or unified whole. [4]

The way the integration was envisioned, the VRS system would generate and/or collect requests for items as the shop guys entered them. These requests would then be shuttled to MYSYS so the procurement department could fill each request. The information about each fulfillment would then be shuttled back to VRS, where it would use the data to update work order parts usage and stock balances.

As the customization and implementation of VRS progressed, I was finally given the green light to get involved with the Winner to work out the nuts-and-bolts of the integration. During a joint planning meeting, I learned that the integration would be facilitated on the VRS side by the Winner's import/export module, which was apparently able to import/export a variety of data formats and do all kinds of wonderful things with that data.

Since MYSYS was custom developed and didn't have a fancy import/export engine, early in the process I set expectations with my client that I would have to do custom development to import/export VRS data. But, because that meant I was starting with basically a blank slate, I could do it "however it works best for the Winner's VRS system." I'm pretty sure I uttered those exact words during the meeting. I just needed to understand exactly what kind of data I would be getting from the engine and what kind of data I needed to send back. According to the person speaking for the Winner at the meeting, the power and flexibility of the import/export engine would make this a very straight-forward project.

[4]"Integrate." Webster's Ninth New Collegiate Dictionary. 1987

Then I started working with the Winner's technical folks. First of all, we wouldn't be using their import/export tool because "it wasn't appropriate for the kind of data we would be exchanging." The bigger problem however, was that it became apparent that the Winner was pretty unclear about the steps in my client's business process, and exactly which of the two systems should handle which of the steps. I worked up some simple process models for them and we came up with preliminary concept for exchanging data, based on using intermediate files dumps (not my idea!) to transfer data between the two systems. We agreed we needed to hammer out more details before I could start coding anything.

Several weeks passed, and nothing happened. Apparently the overall VRS implementation wasn't going well and nobody had been available to work on the VRS-MYSYS integration. Finally, I was contacted by a different person from the Winner about completing the design and we decided it would be best for me to fly down and meet at their office to finalize it.

When I got there, it quickly became clear that the new person had absolutely no knowledge of the original approach, and wanted to go in a completely different direction. The proposal now was for MYSYS to directly access tables in the VRS and read and/or update rows and columns. I had significant reservations about doing this, but the Winners were supposed to be in the lead role on this. If they felt there were sufficient controls in place, then I could certainly accommodate them.

I returned from the trip and notified my client that ditching the first approach and going in a new direction was going to consume more of my time (translation: cost more money). After they agreed, I worked up the details of how the integration would work using this new approach and submitted it to my client and the Winner for approval. Guess what happened? Several more weeks went by without a word from the Winner. Apparently the implementation was now going very badly and, once again, nobody was available to work on the integration.

Finally, someone from the Winner's office — different from the first person, different from the second — got in touch with me. This third person had no knowledge of either of the approaches. I sent him all the documentation I had on the second approach. After reviewing it, he declared that there was "absolutely no way this approach will work." We eventually settled on a third approach, where we would use SQL server tables and event triggers to exchange data between the two systems.

This is what was eventually implemented, approximately two years after that first "joint planning meeting." Over that time, the project almost utterly collapsed. Clearly, what my client thought it purchased was not what it got. With a few years of hindsight, all those involved have been able to piece together the reality.

Apparently the "existing" VRS system my client purchased was a re-write of an older system, and the re-write was only about 50 percent complete when the Winner sold it to my client. We couldn't use the import/export engine because it didn't exist. It was one of the many pieces that hadn't been re-written, and it was never completely clear that the Winner had ever intended to re-write it. To this day, I still don't think it's been completed, and the company that wrote it went out of business. My client had to salvage what it could of the VRS system it ended up with and, in some cases, moved parts of the process to other systems, including MYSYS (which was good for me).

Any time we finish a project and, more importantly, any time we suffer a failure, Steve and I try to perform forensics to figure out what happened and how any problems could have been prevented. Although this wasn't my failure and I was not involved in the RFP process, I still really wanted to know how it could have gone so badly off-track.

From that information I was able to gather, most of the problems went back to the RFP process. The requirements documented in the RFP in many cases were either vague, insufficient, or missed *completely. When I asked how the requirement to integrate with VRS was stated in the RFP, I was told it looked pretty much like this:*

Requirement	System Complies	Does not Comply
Integrates with Purchasing System	Yes	

Obviously, this requirement was, um, lacking some specifics. My client provided absolutely no details about what it meant by "integrates," or even what kind of purchasing system to which it was referring. What's worse, when the Winner responded that, yes, its VRS system could integrate with the purchasing system, my client chose to believe that requirement was now met.

My client made it extremely easy for the Winners to dole out hype, and even more easily swallowed the hook once it was offered. It should have not only provided much more detail about the requirements but, even more importantly, it should have gone to much greater lengths to test and confirm the Winner's claims before accepting them.

My client made it extremely easy for the Winners to dole out hype, and even more easily swallowed the hook once it was offered. It should have not only provided much more detail about the requirements but, even more importantly, it should have gone to much greater lengths to test and confirm the Winner's claims before accepting them. Had my client insisted on seeing the system actually working and integrating with other systems, it would have been able to either confirm that the VRS could do what it was purported to do, or more likely, would have been able to dismiss the Winner's hype as just that, and moved on to a more suitable solution.

Chapter 5: Solving the Wrong Problem

M any years ago, before the Berlin Wall came down, back when the bad guys all wore neatly starched uniforms and pointed their bombs at military targets, I was a spy. No, not the 007 kind of spy; I was a military intelligence analyst and team leader. I know that military intelligence is often considered an oxymoron, but once or twice we actually did something intelligent. Although I can't tell you very much about the details of my job then, I can tell you that during peacetime, military intelligence is often a dull affair and consists primarily of imagination.

"Sir," I might report during a training exercise, "There is an enemy tank battalion on the other side of this hill."

"I can never trust you intelligence weenies," the operations officer would respond with disdain. "How do you know?"

"Because, sir, if you climb the hill and look on the other side, an exercise controller is walking around with a big sign that says: 'I am an enemy tank battalion.'"

OK, maybe it wasn't always that bad, but sometimes it was. On one assignment my team worked with real intelligence concerning real bad guys doing real things. Our mission was stated in broad and general terms. When translated from military speak to natural language it was something like this: Do spy stuff, figure out things about the bad guys, and let us know. So, we did whatever we thought that meant. Shortly after taking the assignment, the "us" in "let us know" expanded to include a newly assigned general. As you might guess, a new general always wants more than the last guy. Shortly after he arrived at his new post, we received a lengthy order that boiled down to: Let us know faster.

We did what all good operations do — military or civilian — when confronted with new orders: We started an IT project to improve the "system" so we could "let them know faster." We spent liberally and installed a fancy new military IT system, which was actually a modest computer in a very large and very rugged box painted camouflage. After months of installation, training, change management, documenting of procedures and the like, we had a system that sped up the "let us know" process by an average of 60 percent. Everybody got a pat on the back and a nice annual review. We were amazing, effective, and all that other good stuff. However, the general's reaction was that it didn't seem any faster to him and we had better go faster still.

Our next response was to "improve the operating model" and "optimize" the system. We embarked on a several-month journey of tuning, training, and various improvements of controls and governance, which achieved an astounding 50-percent further improvement, making our average response time nearly 80-percent faster than our original performance. We were heroes! After all, we had worked many nights and weekends to make such a significant leap in capability. Who wouldn't be happy with that? You guessed it, the general. His response was that he was approving considerable expense and we had spent many months working on that system and still he was seeing no improvement.

I had just read one of my favorite books, *Are Your Lights On?* by Gauss and Weinberg (see the bibliography) and was beginning my journey into systems thinking. I began to wonder if we were solving the wrong problem. After discussing this with my peers, we were able to communicate the suggestion that the general might want to pay us a visit. Some weeks later, he arrived to much fanfare, plenty of formal presentations at map boards, and professionally produced slides and charts. The general was baffled at the end of it all. He tried not to show it and we tried not to notice, but it was clear we had missed the mark and he couldn't even begin to fathom what we had been doing all this time.

Being a smarter-than-average general, he insisted on spending some time "getting to know the troops" without his usual protective layer of senior officers. He spent a few minutes with each of the teams, asking some typical questions and most of the other officers lost interest and congregated around the high-tech equipment for more demonstrations. When he headed to my team, I asked him simply, "General, what is it you want us to do for you?"

He explained, with a clear passion for the mission, that the bad guys had special units. These units were hard to find and were particularly dangerous. In a time of war, the things he needed to do would be in serious jeopardy if we allowed these special units to do their job uninterrupted. He needed us to find these units as quickly as possible so he could attack them early in a battle and thus significantly increase his chances of success. The speed and accuracy of information that was not about these special units wasn't nearly as important. Much of the information we were sending him he could find out elsewhere, but we were the experts on these particular units and he needed us to use that expertise. He had even devised a scheme to prove we had done it during peacetime so he would have confidence that it could be done when it really mattered. He spent several minutes outlining his plan in detail.

We had been solving the wrong problem. Although we had increased our average performance, performance for the only item that mattered to the general had not changed. Fortunately, the general's investment was not a complete loss. Armed with an understanding of the real problem, we were eventually able to deliver what he wanted. He considered the total investment a bargain so we didn't look quite as stupid as we might have.

Communicating Purpose

Solving the wrong problem is probably the most common and devastating issue I encounter. It stems from weaknesses in two executive functions: establishing purpose and facilitating communication. Nobody can thoroughly understand a problem if they don't know the overall goal of the company, department, or project. No matter how many heroes you throw at the problem, if you are solving the wrong one, you cannot succeed. This is exactly what happened on the general's project. An unclear statement of purpose forced us to interpret our mission to the best of our ability. Greater ambiguity leads to greater invention. What you want and what you get in an IT project drift further and further apart.

Greater ambiguity leads to greater invention. What you want and what you get in an IT project drift further and further apart.

Additionally, it must be clear what a successful resolution of the problem really means. If you can't complete the sentence "this problem is successfully resolved when …", you do not fully understand the problem. The general in my story eventually made clear not only what he wanted, but how we could tell if we were delivering it. We were left with a specific timeline. Anything slower than the specified timeframe was useless and we might as well not even deliver the information. Processing in less than the required time gave him more options and we would be rewarded if we continually improved our performance, but only after we had met the no-later-than objective.

The trap for most executives is they assume their team either understands the big picture, or doesn't need to understand it, and — because of their understanding — is only presenting solutions directly related to the purpose of the organization. In reality, IT teams frequently understand neither the purpose nor the strategy of the organization and provide solutions based on their own assumptions about the problem.

Another frequent scenario is a request for a specific technical solution without any information about the problem the requestor is trying to solve. Decision makers might do this for a variety of reasons. They might think they know the technology well enough to design a solution, or maybe they don't want some sales guy talking them into something they don't really want. Being too specific about a solution is just as problematic as being too vague about the problem. The key to mitigating the effect of a solutions-oriented problem statement is to ask, ask, ask. You might try something like, "I understand what you want us to do, but can you give me more insight on how you will know we were successful?"

Many times, asking these kinds of questions converts a request to create an entirely new system into a request for a few simple changes to an existing component, thus avoiding the classic "that's what I asked for, but not really what I wanted" failure. Understanding and communicating purpose — the purpose of the business and the purpose of a proposed IT investment — is critical to success.

Tool: Business Purpose

To avoid solving the wrong problem, Russ and I use a tool we call the business purpose. This is one of the least structured of our tools because it deals with your IT project at the highest level of abstraction. However, it does have some structure. A business purpose is a short narrative — I try to keep mine to a page or less — that describes what the IT investment is all about.

Although brevity is essential, a presentation slide will not do. Overly abbreviated or bullet-list statements can be as ambiguous as rambling prose. Write sentences and put them in paragraphs. A few bullets to make a list of points easier to read is OK, but the bulk of the business purpose should be complete sentences. Trust our years of experience in this regard. Every time we have tried to do this in PowerPoint we have been sorry later in the project.

A business purpose must include all of the interrogatives: who, what, when, where, why, and how. It must also define success. It is extremely important that your answer to the question "why" and your definition of success be testable. You must be able to prove, at the end of the project, that you have achieved the objective and the objective must be clear before you even begin. Because a business purpose is brief and clarity is essential, be careful with your vocabulary. I'll talk more about how vocabulary contributes to solving the wrong problem next; just remember to define or avoid verbiage that is unclear or can be misinterpreted.

Last, your business purpose should be good enough. Perfection is extremely difficult to achieve, especially on the first pass. A good business purpose is difficult to write so don't be too worried about absolute precision. Remember that you can iterate and improve the language as the project proceeds. Beware however, a well-written business purpose serves as the foundation for the rest of the project and changes could have far-reaching effects. Once a project is approved, I prefer to have an executive steering committee, or at least the person or group that approved the project, acknowledge any changes I make to the business purpose.

The following business purpose is an example from a workshop Russ and I give on systems design and project management. The company and project are fictitious, but the problem has been analyzed over the years by hundreds of IT professionals at our workshops, and the business purpose has served us well.

> **Overview:** F&M is a family-owned legal research firm. It maintains a legal library that contains more than 20,000 unique assets in the form of books and publications that are valued at more than $12M. Staff and friends of the firm use the library for research and may check out books. The library is located on the third floor of the F&M main office and all related processes and systems are in close proximity. The library system is (and should be) be limited to the third floor.
>
> The library is suffering unexplained losses totaling as much as $60,000 yearly. Irreplaceable assets are lost, reducing the library's business value. Asset valuation is inaccurate. By not tracking library assets accurately, the

firm believes it is missing out on claiming as much as $100,000 in annual depreciation.

Additionally, the CEO believes that outdated systems are making it more difficult to attract top law school graduates to the firm.

Key Objectives:

Reduce or eliminate unexplained book losses.

Track and report library asset values such that the firm can report the additional $100,000 depreciation.

Implement new technology (such as RFID tags) to demonstrate to hire prospects the firm's willingness to embrace progressive technology.

Complete and implement the new system before the CEO retires at the end of the year.

Related Objectives/Actions:

Implement a system to allow library staff to maintain auditable library asset data.

Include an automated process to send valuation updates to the AcuBill system, with an optional manual certification process to be used by the Auditor.

This project is successful if (in order of priority):

The completed system is implemented before the end of the year.

All related objectives/actions listed above are completed.

Data received by AcuBill from the new system enables the firm to show evidence of library asset depreciation ($100,000 or more).

Asset losses are reduced, and the firm can determine the most recent activity on a lost asset.

Can you find the answers to our six interrogatives: who, what, when, where, why, and how? Cover the list below with your hand or a piece of paper and find them yourself. If you do a good job, you will notice just how many unanswered questions remain. This business purpose is good enough, at least good enough for our workshop; but, a careful examination of the interrogatives will help you to improve any business purpose even your own.

Who = The firm F&M, staff, friends, shareholders, CEO, law school graduates (you might also call them hire prospects), library staff, AcuBill (not a person but a system that is likely to be considered a "who" in the context of this IT project), auditor.

What = The library, research (the result of researching), library system, books and publications (called assets), losses, the value of the library, depreciation, new technology (RFID), library system (current system), new system, auditable asset data, AcuBill system (a thing in this case), data received by AcuBill, recent activity for lost assets.

When = The cycle of depreciation (annual), law school graduations and associated recruitment events, length of time over which $60,000 in assets have been lost, time associated with tracking and reporting, the end of the year, the CEO's retirement, an audit, the transfer of data to AcuBill (frequency, time of day, and duration may be important), showing evidence of asset depreciation, when an asset was acted upon (e.g., check-out, audit, other events).

Where = The geographic location of the F&M office, the third floor of the F&M office, the library, the location of the AcuBill system, work locations of the library staff, layout of the assets in the library, where RFID equipment might be located, electrical power and communications layout that might be needed to operate the library system, the location of audits, the location of valuations, the location of check-out, the layout of the rest of the third floor and proximity of related systems, where graduates are recruited, where the auditor will manually certify transactions.

Why = Unexplained losses totaling $60,000, irreplaceable losses, reduction of the library's business value, inaccurate asset valuation resulting in possible miss of $100,000 depreciation annually, antiquated systems make it difficult to recruit top talent, CEO is retiring (there's more to why this is important, but it is not evident here), desire to automate data movement to AcuBill, desire to have a manual certification process, need to show evidence of change in depreciation, desire to reduce losses, and ability to track recent activity of lost assets (presumably to aid in recovery or collecting compensation, but one should not presume).

How = Maintaining a library and library assets, asset valuation, doing research, checking out books (assets), the process of books being misplaced, tracking library assets, claiming annual depreciation, attracting top graduates, reducing unexplained losses, reporting asset value, reporting depreciation, implementing new technology, demonstrating willingness to embrace progressive technology, CEO retirement, the process of completing the new system, implementing new system, auditing library assets, sending updates to AcuBill (automated), the certification process (manual), showing evidence of depreciation, reducing asset losses, showing recent asset activity.

> *The business purpose becomes a tool for communication, validation, and leveling. It should be a prominent part of any documentation, presentations or marketing.*

The business purpose becomes a tool for communication, validation, and leveling. It should be a prominent part of any documentation, presentations or marketing. Everyone on the project, affected by the project, or near the project should be able to easily quote — from memory or by finding a nearby copy — the key points from the business purpose. I frequently go to meetings where someone asks, "Why are we doing this?" and most often the room is silent.

Don't ever let this happen again on your IT projects. Make sure everyone knows what you are doing and why.

Russ has a particularly effective twist on the business purpose that he has used on at least one project (see the "Sign If You Agree" section in chapter 6). He created a specific purpose statement for each team on his project so the team leader would clearly understand — and was asked to acknowledge — their specific mission. You may find many ways to put this concept into practice. Given the impact solving the wrong problem has, we applaud any efforts to clearly communicate purpose.

Vocabulary

Communication of purpose aside, you are still likely to have a gap in communicating problems because of the radically different vocabulary and perspectives of business operations and IT. We IT people have trouble with even simple business vocabulary. My favorite example is "customer." Imagine a manufacturer that sells products to a final assembly shop, that sells to a regional distributor, that sells to a local distributor, that sells to a delivery firm, that sells to a retailer, that sells to a shopper, who provides the item to the consumer. Depending on how much of the supply chain you own, and where you are in the chain, your definition of customer will vary. In large or complex organizations several of these may be considered customers. To make matters more complex, when the IT department hears "customer" they think of the internal business units they support.

On top of simple, but ambiguous, business terms like "customer," the IT department adds technology-specific terminology and many, many acronyms. "At our SCRUM stand-up meeting, SQA found weaknesses in the object hierarchy and determined that our BW DBMS does not have an adequate XI adapter which will affect both the ETL and our ITIL processes," says your IT liaison during a project review meeting. What on earth are they talking about and why do they want another $100,000 and six weeks on the project plan?

Imagine this scenario: The inside sales team, assuming it needs to specify its requirements in technical terms, provides a bulleted list of features it wants in a new telephone sales application — no business purpose, just a bulleted list of features. The IT team makes assumptions about what the abbreviated or business-specific terminology means and why the sales team wants the application. They prepare to deliver the features. Because they are hip and modern IT people, they don't just build the application; they first develop a prototype to get "sign-off" from the business on the design.

When a prototype is developed, it makes no sense to the sales team because instead of using the sales team's terms, the IT team has adopted "industry standard" language — which means IT techno-babble. Nonetheless, the prototype looks cool and the sales team assumes the IT guys are solving the right problem and know the best way to build a solution. The sales team signs off on the design, making its own assumptions about what might be changeable in the future. When the wrong thing is delivered, the teams go through the cycle again; this time with a higher level of frustration and distrust.

Breaking this cycle is easier than you might think. The executive sponsor of the initiative must ensure that both teams communicate in terms of delivered business value and not in specifications or technical documents. In this example, it might mean that the sales team tells the IT team: "Our telesales staff averages thirty-five completed sales calls per representative per shift. We want improved tools that will enable our existing staff to complete three more calls per representative per shift. This increase will contribute $4.5 million annually to the top line without any cost increase except the implementation and support of the new tools. Our internal hurdle rate is 16 percent and we want a payback in one year. If you can build it in 12 months for less than $3.8 million, we can ask for the capital to fund the project. Here is the research on the current tools and telesales process that shows where we might gain efficiency …"

> *Your IT team may not be used to talking in those terms, but those are the terms in which other business investments are made.*

Your IT team may not be used to talking in those terms, but those are the terms in which other business investments are made. IT should be no different. In addition, this kind of communication makes it much easier to measure the right thing (chapter 7). Solving the right problem means communicating in terms of the problem not the solution.

Insider-speak

As you may have noted from our author biographies, I work for a large, well-known consumer packaged goods company. To do my job, I regularly visit our operations around the world. A typical visit includes a briefing on the market, product mix, type of customers served, competitors, and plans for the future. This is followed by visits to retailers, wholesalers, and distributors along with tours of manufacturing, distribution, and other company-owned facilities.

At the time of this writing, one of my daughters is a student of linguistics and Asian studies at the University of Texas at Austin. I was scheduled to visit our operation in Thailand and she asked to accompany me. She paid for her own airfare and joined me to learn how we do business in Asia and get to know the Thai people. As you can imagine, I was thrilled to show off our business to my daughter and she was equally excited to see how it all worked.

The corporate business language is English. Although many of our associates in Thailand speak other languages, particularly their own, for a manager to rise to a senior level, they must have a fairly good command of English. Given that my Thai is limited to a smile and a bow, this makes things easier for me. All of the presentations and discussions would be in English and, for the most part, in well-spoken English (mine being the exception). My daughter and I arrived Monday morning rested and prepared to learn about our business in Thailand.

The presentations were thorough but not overwhelming, the visual displays useful and meaningful, and the discussion robust. My daughter listened intently. After a fast-moving two hours we took a snacks and beverage break (my favorite part of working for a consumer packaged goods company's international business). I met my daughter in the hallway outside the conference room and with great expectations asked her what she thought of our business in Thailand. The conversation went something like this:

"So what do you think?"

"About what?" she asked.

"About all of it, our business, the market opportunities, our distribution channels, our products," I replied a little confused.

"Honestly, I haven't understood a word you're saying."

"Oh, is the Thai accent a problem for you?"

"No, that's not a problem," she replied. "I don't understand a word they are saying and I don't understand a word you are saying. I mean you, the guy I've lived with all my life. What on earth have you been talking about?"

"Um…our business, it has just been the basics so far."

"Well, your business has a very particular vocabulary. I have understood none of the nouns and very few of the verbs. Is there going to be a time where you use words — and definitions — I might find in a standard college dictionary?"

I was stunned. The presentations were really basic. For a little while, I forgot what this chapter is all about. Just because I understood the vocabulary doesn't mean it was understandable by anyone else. For those of us initiated in the language of our business, the conversation was clear, but the clarity was limited to a specific group of people and an outsider was, frankly, baffled.

Tool: Project Dictionary

How do you solve the vocabulary problem? Simple, maintain a project dictionary. My preference is to keep a corporate dictionary for terminology used anywhere in your business then supplement it with terms specific to your project. Once the project is complete, consider adding project dictionary entries into the corporate dictionary. Depending on the size of the project you can keep a project dictionary in hand-written notes in an easy-to-access notebook, or you can publish it on an internal website. However you store it, a dictionary entry is simple: word, definition, and an example if helpful. That's it.

As you might suspect, Russ and I didn't write this book all in one sitting. Chapters that were nearly complete waited while the demands of our own IT projects took our time and attention. Several weeks after its completion, I returned to re-read this chapter and was happy to note that I had practiced what I preach. I spent much of the preceding week wrestling with some particularly difficult issues on a current project.

Much of the difficulty revolved around the words we use. In a twist of the story about my daughter baffled by specific business vocabulary, I was working with several different business units that all used the same vocabulary but had different meanings for the same words. Sometimes these differences were subtle and caused misunderstanding that was difficult to notice and then even tougher to track to a root cause.

My team identified several such terms that were causing serious problems. Since we needed to write a white paper stating our strategic position in a particular area, I took the opportunity to insert a section specifically for definitions. These definitions were presumably so that people reading the white paper would understand how we were using the words in that context. However, by publishing these definitions, we were establishing our meaning of the words. This will allow us to return to the definitions for clarity or as a starting point for discussions. Over time, the definitions will work their way into other material and a common understanding (at least in the context of our project) will emerge.

You might notice from my description that a simple project dictionary doesn't exist. Given the scope of my team, which spans many individual projects, a published definitions list would either be ignored or would insult one or another individual project team. Nonetheless, a dictionary is still needed and we had to find a way to develop and distribute key definitions in order to facilitate overall progress. The position paper, which would be widely read based on the topic, gave us a medium through which to deliver the most critical definitions in both an acceptable and effective manner. In your projects, you may have to find a creative way to make definitions reach the right audience. Be wary of a nicely formatted document or website that nobody ever reads.

Chapter 6:
Using the Wrong People

I n keeping with the spirit of the previous chapter I offer several personal definitions. I define "state-of-the-art" as: a technique or practice that a limited number of organizations have trialed that provides a leap forward in some way and is likely to become the standard way of doing things in the future. "State-of-the-practice" is the set of best practices used regularly by high-performing organizations. Or said another way, those practices to which we aspire that are reasonably within our grasp to achieve. "State-of-the-military" is a set of practices in an organization, such as the U.S. military, that are institutionalized, worst-practices proudly executed with precision and flair for more than 100 years.

Many years of direct experience with the state-of-the-military has provided me with numerous lessons that sometimes — but not always — resulted in physical injury as well as failing to meet the objectives. Using the wrong people is a long standing worst-practice of the U.S. Army in particular. For those of you unfamiliar with the U.S. military, I submit some opinions formed from inside the organization. The U.S. Air Force recruits the brightest young men and women. Those who are not smart enough to survive the constant written and oral examinations, but who still want a military career, depart the Air Force and join the Army. The U.S. Marine Corps recruits the most physical and motivated young men and women. Those who cannot handle the physical or emotional stress, but still want a military career, escape to the Army. The U.S. Navy recruits the most adventurous and versatile young men and women. Those who cannot swim, or cannot operate in the constraints of a sea-borne vessel find their way to the U.S. Army. The U.S. Army recruits all living young men and women not otherwise engaged in another military service (including sometimes those whose status as "living" may be in question).

Turning the Wrong People into the Right People

As a result of a string of decisions — which I staunchly refuse to call bad decisions regardless of how true that might seem in retro-spect — I found myself a military intelligence analyst in the U.S. Army. By lucky circumstance, or providence, I was assigned to one of the most prestigious operations, working on real live spy stuff, on one of the most difficult assignments, with the brightest of the U.S. Army recruits and veterans. In real terms, I was in a small office with a dozen newly assigned, clueless troops.

These troops had been selected for this position through a rig-orous process. First, they had to have a high score on the Army entrance test (not a particularly grueling examination in itself). If the local recruiter did not have enough recruits who passed the test, exceptions were granted, usually supported by incorrectly entered test scores — unintentionally, no doubt. Next, these recruits had to endure military basic training, which means that the truly bright ones found a way out. Then, they had to obtain a top-secret clear-ance. For most Americans there is only so much trouble you can get into in 18 years, and having a clearance is no indication you will be good a job that requires a clearance. (I submit the U.S. Senate Intelligence Committee as proof.) Finally, these recruits under-went advanced individual training in their chosen career field. It is important to know that the description of the career field was, for the most part, classified and neither the recruits nor their recruiters had any idea what they would be doing.

The military in general, and the U.S. Army in particular, is fond of cramming three hours of material into a two-week course. This rig-orous pace meant that few students failed. The success rate was also reinforced by the high degree of motivation for both the students (if you don't pass this class, you get to be a cook) and the instructors (if you don't have a good pass ratio, you get sent to the worst assignment available). From this pool of trained soldiers, the Army Personnel Office used a sophisticated assignment mechanism that ensured people who spoke German went to Korea and people who spoke Korean went to New Jersey. The team I joined had not been chosen completely at random, but any effort at selecting the right people for the job was not apparent through casual observation.

It took several months for new people to really learn their tasks and, as might be expected, we each settled in at a different level of skill. I had the pleasure of working with seasoned veterans who were very good at their jobs and some of the new team members quickly developed similar talent. This meant that despite the Army's attempt at getting all the wrong people in all the wrong places, we had a team that performed extremely well. That is, all except for Kelly.

Our office worked in shifts. The senior management team worked a regular work week, allowing them to make regular contact with the rest of the team. A permanent team worked the night shift. This was a skeleton crew of capable but less competitive team members whose main role would be to call for help if something critical happened at night. The rest of the group was broken evenly into two sub-teams rotating between day and evening shifts and covering the weekends. Kelly and I were assigned to opposite rotating sub-teams.

My shift began noticing that when Kelly's shift worked in the evenings or on weekends — when they didn't have support from the day-shift veterans — errors were made. We started by adjusting misfiled information and correcting minor analysis and moved to cancelling intelligence reports that contained errors of fact or faulty analysis. I was young, very competitive, hot-headed, and particularly good at this kind of work. Naturally, I made it clear that my shift noticed the incompetence of the opposing shift and was tired of fixing their errors. It was obvious that the problem was Kelly. All of the incompetence traced to her. After a particularly frustrating weekend and some very unkind remarks directed at Kelly, my boss took me aside and explained the realities of military life.

First, you can't fire anyone in the military. Gross negligence, illegal activity, and the repeated and knowing breaking of regulations could pave the path toward a dishonorable discharge; however, incompetence was never sufficient justification for removal. Moving or removing a soldier assigned to your unit was nearly impossible. Second, as a result of the first reality, Kelly was staying on the team without regard to how much I complained. Third, since my boss had considerable latitude in making assignments, he could send me outside to guard the flag pole if I wasn't nicer to the team members. Fourth, he was assigning the problem of making Kelly a functioning member of the team to me.

Although I was not, Kelly was a genuinely nice person. She was bright and cheerful except when engaged in the work she had been assigned. Fortunately for both Kelly and me, she had a shift-mate who was also a nice person and volunteered to help discover the cause of Kelly's incompetence and assist with a solution. With his help, we realized the obvious. Our job was military intelligence. This meant we dealt daily with tanks and trucks and artillery, bombers and helicopters, patrol boats and battleships. We read Jane's Defense Weekly and argued over whether the published effective range of a particular howitzer was the actual effective range. Kelly, on the other hand, was a girl.

We had several women on our team, but Kelly wasn't your typical Army woman. She had played dolls and tea while the neighbor boys were playing war. She lived a life absent of trucks and tanks until, for some reason, she decided to join the Army. Her only experience with weaponry was in basic training. The only other military gear she remotely understood was gear she had personally come into contact with since joining the Army. She was functionally illiterate when it came to military stuff. She was definitely the wrong person for the job.

Fortunately, for me in particular but also for her, this was a correctable condition. I had a friend who was an artillery mechanic, and one of the most impressive machines in any army is a self-propelled howitzer (a really big gun on a tank chassis). We arranged for Kelly to visit with the artillery guys. I say guys in this case because women didn't serve in front-line units in those days. Needless to say, they were very enthusiastic about explaining all of their gear to a friendly, 19-year-old, single female. Kelly went on to visit tank units, infantry units, and support units of various kinds. At the end of her training in military stuff, she probably knew more than any of us about how all those things worked and how they were used in combat. It was amazing how quickly she became one of our best analysts.

I want two points to come through from this story. First, the effect of using the wrong people is widespread; and second, if you are stuck with the wrong people, make them into the right people or find other ways to compensate. You may have noticed how Kelly's poor performance affected the immediate team, but did you notice the ripple effect? Kelly's performance caused frustration and embarrassment to her own shift, and extra work and frustration on my shift as we compensated for her errors. The day-shift people were obviously also catching and correcting her errors spending time on tasks they would normally not have done. The unit as a whole lost credibility as we frequently cancelled or revised our reports and analysis.

> *On the surface it would appear that you should be able to swap people without significant impact on your project. This is generally true if you want to maintain a high rate of failure.*

Sometimes, as in this case, you are stuck with the wrong people. Rather than compensating by overworking your heroes, making these wrong people into the right people or minimizing the effect they have on the project is usually worth the effort. In my many years since being a hot-headed shift leader, I have grown to appreciate that almost every team member has value, but placing them properly is the important part of the work.

People Are Not Fungible Assets

Whether a project employs an in-house team or uses outsourced staff for some or all of the work, the failure rate remains the same. On the surface it would appear that you should be able to swap people without significant impact on your project. This is generally true if you want to maintain a high rate of failure. If, however, you would like to shift that trend, a focus on using the right people becomes much more important. When considering the option to outsource some, or all, of your project, the question is not, "Should I outsource?" it is, "Where are the right people?"

Systems design and development professionals have as much as an order of magnitude difference in individual productivity[5]. That productivity advantage is usually limited to skill or experience in one type of work or one particular technology. Given the wide range of productivity, the effort of finding and keeping the right team is more than recovered during the life of your project.

Organizations in which hero syndrome is strong use this difference in productivity to justify hiring and retaining heroes. However, heroic effort is not what makes the difference in productivity. These productivity differences are measures of the same task performed in the same timeframe with the same resources. Heroism is not a factor. Your heroes are also bound to their area of expertise. It doesn't matter how hard they work, if your hero cannot do the work, they will not be able to save your project.

Unfortunately, this also means that having the right people for one project doesn't necessarily mean you have the right people for the next project. When well-managed, outsourcing can allow you to shift technology or skill-specific talent into your organization when you need it and out when the need is no longer there. Doing this requires active management of those people and ways to ensure you always have the right people. The people you keep in the organization then need more general skills such as project management,

[5] DeMarco, Tom and Lister, Timothy, *Peopleware*, 1987, Dorset House, pp 44-46

systems integration, support, testing, etc. If this is your outsourcing plan, you have to manage your internal team just as well as you manage your contractors. The programmers who built all of those cool systems for Marketing in a tool that was popular ten years ago need to go unless they have developed into a skilled deployment or quality assurance managers.

Using the Right People

It is easy to think of the wrong people as people like Kelly who, before she was given the proper foundational experience, made frequent errors and clearly performed below an acceptable level. However, the goal is not just to avoid using the wrong people, but to use the right people. The right people are the best performers your project can afford. Almost always that really means the best performers available in the market, because the top performers produce more than their marginal difference in cost.

Your goal on every project should be to staff it with superstars — not heroes, but the best consistent performers. Your other option is unknowns who have raw talent and will become superstars after a couple of successful projects. Were I to guess, I would say your team is composed of very dedicated mediocre performers. Some of those can be trained to be top performers (chapter 9), but most are working at their best now and their best falls into the middle of the pack.

Using the wrong people affects estimates of the effort required to complete the project. Because of the large differences in individual productivity, the wrong people cannot possibly give you the right estimate.

Using the wrong people affects estimates of the effort required to complete the project. Because of the large differences in individual productivity, the wrong people cannot possibly give you the right estimate. If your IT initiatives are typically very small and you work with the same group of people, you can come to know the individual productivity of the members of your team. From this, you can develop realistic estimates, as long as the work in question is similar to work the team has already done. Even if you use the wrong people, consistency in size and type of project will help you develop a baseline from which you can estimate and ultimately improve.

If your IT initiatives are typically very large — say you have 30-90 people working on essentially the same task — productivity will tend toward an industry or company average. In this case, reasonable estimates are possible regardless of the makeup of the team. However, most IT projects of any great import require a medium-sized team, and team members shift in both participation and role from project to project. When you outsource, this is exacerbated by a constantly shifting capability base. The "popular" skills are always changing. To mitigate the risks associated with change in market demand, smart outsourcing suppliers move their people to prevent them from becoming obsolete. Even if some of the team remains the same from project to project, almost any personnel shift will overlook team experience as a significant factor in developing a reliable estimate.

Not only does the difference in individual productivity wreak havoc on your project estimates, the fact such differences exist means you really want to have the high productivity people on your team. As I mentioned before, even at twice the cost, someone who can produce at ten times the rate is a bargain. However, people at wildly different productivity levels are not fungible. They cannot be replaced in an equal manner. If you assign a high performer to your project, then lose that person to illness, unless you can find an equal or greater productivity replacement, your project estimates are worthless. Significant reductions in individual productivity can have a huge impact. Thus, if your plan depends on high-productivity people who are difficult to replace, your risk-management plan (chapter 8) must include the risk of losing those non-fungible assets.

In a perfect world, you can identify and hire or assign the right people to your project. Unfortunately, simply identifying a high-performing individual is difficult. A disciplined manager who has worked with a team over several projects will have a good idea of the relative capabilities of his people. However, even this requires you to have a good manager and to have that manager's experience with the team span several projects. I have found a successful project manager with a thick Rolodex to be an invaluable resource. Internal tracking of individual productivity is difficult, may result in measuring the wrong things (chapter 7), and could lead to unhealthy internal competition. If you have a regular exercise program (chapter 9), you may use a training exercise or a friendly competition to help evaluate the current productivity of your team members. Sometimes just asking around will give you a pretty good idea of the relative productivity of your team members. For contractors, new hires, or transfers from other parts of your organization I recommend an audition.

Right People, Wrong Team

Russ writes: Steve has focused much of his talk on individuals, but there's another important aspect to this problem. Just because all the individual members of a project team are the "right" people, does not automatically guarantee that they will form the "right" team.

As several NFL team owners have demonstrated time and again in the age of free-agency, collecting the very best talent available does not ensure this talent will perform well together. I have personally experienced projects where two superstars spent more time tearing each other to pieces than they did contributing to the success of the project.

However, this point really hit home with me in my personal life. Every year for the last five years, I have gone on an annual fishing trip with a group of friends. Because the trip has constants (i.e., packing/preparation, duration/schedule, location), variables (weather, fishing success, composition of the team), and results (how much fun we had, how much we're looking forward to going next year, everyone survived), I've been able to reflect on it *as a repeatable experiment and observe how the variables have affected the success/results.*

This table shows a breakdown of how I would rate each trip:

Fishing Success	Weather	Composition of Team	Fun (5 is best)
Good	OK	Russ, Pete, Matt, Kyle, Jeff	3
Great	OK	Russ, Pete, Matt, Kyle, Ben, Skippy	3
Good	Poor	Russ, Pete, Matt, Kyle	4
Mediocre	Poor	Russ, Pete, Matt, Doug	1
Bad	OK	Russ, Pete, Matt, Kyle	5

The conclusion I reached was pretty obvious: In terms of success, the weather and fishing success was nearly irrelevant. People made the biggest difference. But why? The people in the ideal team are not life-long best friends and don't often see each other. Actually, these trips are the only time Kyle and I have ever spent any time together, so obviously familiarity isn't a major factor here.

I think the factor revealed itself on the drive up on our last trip. Being the risk manager that I am, I dutifully checked the pressure on the boat trailer tires right before I left, and inflated them to their proper levels. 45 minutes into our 10-hour drive, the ominous sound of metal on pavement notified us that one of our trailer tires had blown. What happened next was the revelation. There are probably 20 individual steps involved in changing a tire (including finding the spare, finding the jack, and pumping up the flat spare), which we accomplished in less than 15 minutes (yes, I noted how long it took). In that 15-minute timeframe, there was barely a moment when one of the four of us was not doing something. All four of us understood the steps, when they needed to be executed, and what step each of us should be doing next. For example, while one was jacking up the trailer another was filling the spare. What was really impressive was how little talking there was and that none of us "took charge." We all knew what needed to be done and each was able to anticipate what the others would do and chose the next task accordingly.

When we were all back in the truck and continuing on our way, there was some light joking about my possibly over inflating the tires, but nobody made me feel bad. It was just something that happened and got resolved without drama. This to me was another great indication that the team had gelled. One member might have made a mistake that was potentially detrimental to the rest, but everyone simply accepted the consequences and moved on, without any finger-pointing or long-term effect.

This is what Steve would call a gelled team: a team that is greater than the sum of its parts. Steve and I are a clearly a gelled team. Each of us knows the other's strengths and weaknesses, and can easily anticipate what the other will (and will not) do next, minimizing the time we spend on explaining our plans and actions to each other. Also, when one of us screws up, we both work to correct the damage (if any), briefly discuss how we could prevent the screw up in the future, and then put the matter to rest.

When you look to choose the right people, you have to take the team on which they will be working into consideration. As a project manager with an accounting background, I would love to simply plug "has this skill" guy into "needs this skill team," but in reality that doesn't always work.

Gelled Teams

Russ and I have been part of several gelled teams. The problem with a gelled team is that once you have been a part of one — a group that is truly greater than the sum of its parts — you spend the rest of your life looking for such teams. Unfortunately, gelled teams are few and far between. I wish I could tell you we held the secrets of creating a gelled team, but neither of us is able to prescribe a formula guaranteed to create such a team.

As Russ points out, having the right people is critical, but how do you know which people are the right people? Two things have been common to all of our gelled teams and on any I have observed: diversity and compatibility. When forming a team, look for ways to introduce diversity of thought, approach, background, and perspective. In the U.S. these days diversity means your team has one person whose heritage is Asian, one African, one European, and one Latin. Sometimes this can work, but if each of these people has the same thinking style, training, background, and approach, you don't really have much diversity. Russ' best fishing team may not appear very diverse on the surface, but they each bring different styles and perspectives that improve the group overall.

Compatibility means that the team members can work together. Since the team needs to be diverse, compatibility does not mean uniformity. The team members must have a high tolerance for styles and approaches very different from their own, specifically within the team. The team must be devoid of individual politics, hidden agendas, or personality conflicts. Some people just don't get along.

> *Compatibility means that the team members can work together. Since the team needs to be diverse, compatibility does not mean uniformity.*

Although most people can be polite and professional when working together, the team cannot gel if one member rubs another member the wrong way.

In our experience, the process of gelling is surprisingly quick. If you have been working with some intensity on a team for a week and the team hasn't gelled, chances are it won't. Many times I have seen team-building exercises, collaborative tools, and other team-working techniques significantly improve productivity and quality on teams; however, I have never seen them turn a regular team into a gelled team. Having the right people on the team appears to be the one critical factor.

Tool: The Audition

Interviews, particularly phone interviews are practically useless. If you are just trying to find out if a candidate is lying about their basic skills you can probably do that in an interview. For this case, just give a few questions to your Human Resources group and let them weed out the liars. Candidates who are worth 15 minutes of your time on the phone should come in for an audition. If you want to weed them out in advance, ask them to send a portfolio of representative work. Setting up a good audition takes a little effort. You have to decide what you need to measure and how to measure it. I like to test skill, speed, quality, and fit.

If you are testing skill on a QA specialist or software developer, give them a problem to solve and the tools to solve it and leave them alone until they work out a solution. I have done auditions where someone watches while the candidate works out the solution. I don't recommend this. They are most likely going to be working on these kinds of problems in a cubicle on their own. Replicate an environment where you can measure their skill by itself. Give them the option of asking for help if something in the problem is unclear, or they would like additional materials. You might even describe the basic audition parameters in advance so they can bring their own materials. For example, if you are looking for a Java developer to work on systems integration, let them know they will be writing a short Java program, module, or interface; let them know what development environment they will be using; and explain that they may bring any tools they think appropriate.

Observing how someone responds to a skills evaluation of this kind (not during the work but before and after) can provide a great perspective that you don't get from an interview. However, the only thing you have tested thus far is skill and speed. A great way to test quality and fit is to hold a peer review[6] of the finished work with your team. The candidate's ability to interact during a review, to handle criticism, and to contribute to group thinking will be exposed without your having to rely on their story-telling skills, which is the limit of a traditional interview.

For help-desk specialists, facilitators, infrastructure managers, and other positions where a specific individual task is difficult to devise, create a scenario and use your team members as actors. You might

[6] Freedman, Daniel P. and Gerald M. Weinberg. *Handbook of Walkthroughs, Inspections and Technical Reviews: Evaluation Programs, Projects, and Products.* Third Edition. New York: Dorset House, 1990.

consider adding some hidden agendas that are representative of your business customers or using terminology that is ambiguous or has a specific definition in your business. How a candidate handles a lifelike scenario will tell you much about their skill, speed, and fit. You can review the quality of the outcome or solution in a group review session or even just among yourselves if you prefer. My recommendation is to review quality in an open fashion to see how a candidate reacts to criticism and if they can find creative solutions to issues identified by the review team. Remember too that the best audition delivers a combination of skill, speed, quality, and fit. Fast but poor-quality work is not usually considered a good thing. You have to determine which audition produced the balance best suited to your project.

The Right People

Sometimes you can't easily identify the right people going into your initiative, but you can almost always identify the wrong people while your project is "in flight." By measuring the right things (chapter 7) and avoiding ostrichism (chapter 11) you should be able to observe where your current team is not producing, as well as where you are getting more than expected. On too many projects I have seen people who are obviously wrong for their role continued to be used, to the detriment of the project. Everyone is good at something, but if that something is not what they are doing on your IT initiative, find a replacement.

This is particularly important with consultants or staff-augmentation outsourcing. Ensure your contracts and agreements allow you to replace under-performing or mismatched personnel. Work with your management team to allow people to try new things or stretch into new roles, fail, and return to a former role without shame and with the option of trying something new again if the root cause of failure is identified and corrected. This will give you the flexibility to attempt a good fit and adjust along the way. You don't want your projects caught carrying unproductive or even destructive individuals.

Part of having the right people is using them in the right way. There is an economic principle called Ricardo's Law of Comparative Advantage[7] which, when applied to IT work, boils down to: Everybody should do what they do best even if their second-best skill is better than someone else's best skill. I'll use a simple example. A project manager has three people on their project:

- Sue, whose strongest skill is integration. She is also better than Ken and Win at development.

- Ken, whose strongest skill is testing. He is also better than Sue at integration and better than Win at development.

- Win, whose strongest skill is development. He can also do integration.

Assuming your need for all three skills is simultaneous, Sue should integrate, Ken should test, and Win should develop — even though Win is the worst at development. It is still his best skill and your total productivity will be higher with him doing what he does best. I often see organizations try to create renaissance men out of technical specialists. Annual reviews focus on improving weaknesses and broadening experience instead of focusing on where natural talent and experience are strongest. If you are training general managers or strategists or enterprise architects who will have to deal with a wide range of issues, your emphasis might cover more topics. Even then, I submit that you should train only those whose best skills are as generalists. Your specialists need to specialize.

Compare your team to a national Olympic team. Your goal is to win individual and group medals. You invest in top talent and a great coaching team. For a very few, you might suggest cross-training, but most focus on one particular area. Your sprinters do not learn to platform dive and only those who work well on a precision team train in synchronized swimming. If a runner has proven time and time again that they cannot pass the baton in relays but they always win individual events, you do not waste your time training on baton passing when you have others who are good at it.

I had a friend who was born outside of the United States, but

[7] Ricardo, David. *On The Principles of Political Economy and Taxation.* 1817

attended college in the U.S. and like many, decided to stay and build a career. His English was excellent, but his accent was nearly impossible to understand. He had a quick mind and was sure to understand instructions, designs, strategies, or plans and could build pretty much anything his team could imagine. Conveying ideas in words, however, was not his strong suit. He left several organizations that, with good intentions, asked him to focus on building his communications skills. He intuitively understood that their failure to use him where he was best meant they were doing the same with others, which would lead to overall project failure. He wanted to be part of successful projects and so gravitated to organizations that asked him to learn new computer languages, develop complex components, and hone his skills in rapidly building software at world-class quality. This was where he excelled. Asking him to verbally explain a system component in a meeting was a waste of everyone's time.

Using Ricardo's Law doesn't mean you can't train your team to do other things or that you should not keep them strong on basic skills in which everyone in the industry should maintain competence (chapter 9). But don't waste their time on areas where they have no talent and no interest. Exceptions such as Kelly, who could not move from where she was assigned not withstanding, make sure you have a place for your team members with rock-star talent that does not require them to do something different to be acceptable to the organization or to move to higher levels of responsibility or skill.

Outsourcing Options

Outsourcing has become an increasingly popular way to get the right people when you need them only for a limited time. Even in light of some major outsourcing blunders, organizations continue to outsource because of the value on paper. If you can turn the on-paper advantage of outsourcing into real project success, you are ahead of the typical outsourcing crowd. Our caution against believing the hype (chapter 4) applies here. Trust your outsourcer to provide the right resources, but verify they are the right resources before you begin.

I have a friend in London who outsources several projects to a software firm in Bangalore, a common arrangement these days. But, he does something that isn't so common: He travels to Bangalore every several years and personally interviews scores of candidates for his team. His software partner lines up all of the best candidates and he selects a few best-fit candidates to introduce to his projects. He brings on more candidates than he needs and, after several months, sends those who really weren't such a good fit back to the firm.

This process acts as an extended audition. For a short time he has some of the wrong people, but he can be absolutely sure that the final group is made up of the right people. He works his talented team very hard, but provides them with opportunities to develop stronger skills and build their value in the marketplace. As they improve their skills, some return to the vendor to be supervisors or join other projects. The whole process draws the best candidates onto a team that avoids most of the blunders mentioned in this book and therefore has an outstanding success rate. Everyone wins and my friend gets only the best technologists on his team.

Wrong People Challenges

Sometimes the wrong people are on your team, and there is absolutely nothing you can do about it. Maybe you're restricted to using the same in-house resources, or maybe these people are on the team for political reasons. Either way, you're stuck. In this situation, there are several things you can do to mitigate the risk. First, consider places to allot extra resources to compensate for their shortcomings. This could be some combination of several different skills including quality assurance, management, or technical help. Short-term outsourcing or limited on-site hourly contractors can fill gaps in your technical team if you can ensure you get the right people from your vendor.

Another option is to look for ways to modify the solution to compensate. Although this may sound like an extreme measure, in a small organization with limited resources, it may be your only choice. An in-house development project that dictates a specific technology has no chance to succeed if your team consists of all experts in a completely different technology. Heated religious battles over technology may ensue but, in this case, the senior management team must match the technology with the existing skill set to increase the chances for success. They must make actual and measured business return-on-investment the primary reason for selecting a particular technology for a project.

One obstacle to identifying the right people are the know-it-alls. They might be on your staff, but know-it-alls are also prevalent in consulting firms. As Davy Crocket was known to say, "It ain't bragging if it's true." The question is: How do you know if it is true? Simple, trust but verify. Don't let either your consultants or your internal staff fool you. Look for those

> *Look for those who seem to have a pet technology or singular focus. These folks will sound wise but always guide you toward the same solution.*

who seem to have a pet technology or singular focus. These folks will sound wise but always guide you toward the same solution. Give them a test. Ask your consultants — and internal team — to propose solutions to a business problem for which a best-practice solution already exists. Measuring their answers against the standard will tell you more about what they really know. You want people who are passionate and informed about your business or people with real skill in a specific area, not people who are know-it-alls. Trust but verify.

Sign If You Agree

Russ writes: As an independent consultant, I am never not looking for the next opportunity; the perfect blend of the kind of work I like to do, tackling the kind of problem I love to tackle. Several years ago I was presented a nearly ideal scenario. I was brought in by "the company" to be the project manager in charge of a multi-phase, multi-year contract to develop an entirely new application. Additionally, because the company was relatively small, one of my first jobs would be to hand-pick the 30-40 people who would make up the project team. What could be better than tackling an exciting and new challenge with the help of people mostly of my own choosing?

One of the unique aspects of the project was that the company's customer would neither own nor provide us with the data the application would manage. Instead, the company would act as collector and steward of the data, meaning it would make the business arrangements with the organizations that owned the data. Those organizations would provide us with the data, and we would open "portals" of that data to the customer.

The company possessed enough foresight to engage me before the project got started, which enabled me to begin assembling the team ahead of time. That was when reality stealthily reached out and smacked me upside the head. Remember I said I could choose most of the team? I was informed that both the wireless communication and data collection arrangements and would be done by new employees, whom I'll respectively call Mr. Black and Mr. Blue, brought in by the CEO of the company. I had experience with neither of these people and almost nothing upon which to evaluate their abilities, other than the CEO's word. Still, I was confident they would be suitable for the job, and gathered the rest of my team just as the project got underway.

I strongly believe that the key to success is clearly defining exactly what "success" means, and making sure that each person understands and is committed to that success (chapter 5). Once I divided the project into functional areas, I assigned a team to each area and one team leader for each team. I then wrote a one-pager for each team leader, defining exactly what the team needed to provide to the project (why, what, and by when) to be successful. The page also included a signature block at the bottom to acknowledge that they knew and understood what was *expected of them and their team. I asked each team leader to sign and return it to me.*

I figured each team leader's reaction to this would tell me what to expect from each team, and it did. Every team leader took my request seriously, asked a few questions, signed the paper, and returned it to me within a week ... except for two leaders. Mr. Blue lost track of his, so I printed another one for him, and asked him about it several times. He never signed it. Mr. Black treated the whole thing as a silly, time-wasting exercise and gave me the classic "Yeah, sure, whatever" reaction before hastily signing it and returning it to me. I doubt either one of them ever read it.

Both of those reactions were immediate red flags: Based on their reactions, early on I had identified their roles as potential risk areas in the project. I wasn't sure what I could do about it, but at least I knew early. No asset is more valuable than time when trying to mitigate risk.

In Mr. Black's case, the situation resolved itself pretty easily. Immediately after my "Yeah, sure ..." discussion with him, I contacted an associate of one of the team members and asked if, hypothetically, I had an opening on the team for a wireless communication expert, would he be able to jump in on short notice, and he said yes. So now I had my contingency plan in place should Mr. Black fail to deliver. Sure enough, a few weeks into the project Mr. Black had become involved in "a more strategic project" for the company and was no longer available to assist my team. I thanked him for his efforts, called in my contingency guy, and had him producing for me within a week. Problem solved. (And yes, Mr. Contingency signed the one-pager!)

Mr. Blue was a far more difficult challenge. As the project progressed, it became clear that a) he was going to struggle to produce, b) he was going to stay in that role whether I wanted him or not, and c) he was critical to the success of the project. Because I couldn't simply go to the CEO and ask for him to be replaced or augmented, I had to rely on communicating clearly what Mr. Blue was (and wasn't) contributing to the team. During our weekly project status meetings, which the CEO attended, I made sure that the project Gantt chart clearly showed Mr. Blue's contribution to the critical path, and what would be affected if he failed to deliver. I also devised a separate one-page green/yellow/red report showing the details of Mr. Blue's specific tasks and goals.

Every week, the report would be less green and more yellow/red, and there was nothing I could do about it. However, by showing very clearly to the CEO both the problem at hand and its affect on the project, I effectively left it up to him to choose to solve it (or not). I had to because I didn't have the authority to do it myself. Nevertheless, I repeatedly discussed it with the CEO, and each time he assured me Mr. Blue would come through in the end.

Ultimately, this approach didn't solve the problem. The project fell short in delivering the data that was originally promised, and not just because of Mr. Blue. We ended up approaching the customer and "coming clean" on our difficulties and asked them for their assistance. Once they "shared our pain" on how difficult the data collection was, they were willing to adjust the goals of the project and reduce the amount of data that was ultimately required.

You never get to hand-pick every member of your team, and sometimes you're simply stuck with a dud or two. However, the sooner you can determine who the duds are and identify them as a risk to the success of the project, the more time you'll have to work around them.

Sometimes the best mitigation is to simply replace them, but real-life politics often make that difficult, if not impossible. When mitigation is beyond your authority, communicating the situation to people who are in authority might be your best course of action.

And when all else fails, sometimes you simply have no choice but to adjust your goals accordingly. Pigs will never lay eggs, no matter how many reports you show the farmer on how far behind your egg production is. If pigs are all you have, then maybe bacon should be on the menu instead.

Chapter 7: Measuring the Wrong Things

Everybody nods when I say "you get what you measure" but hardly anyone changes what they measure in order to get what they want. Since this book is about IT project failure, I will assume you want your IT projects to be a success. The most common measure of success for public companies is the rate of return for their investments. You can measure this as various forms of return-on-investment, internal-rate-of-return, etc. Here's a test. For the IT projects underway in your organization 1) have you defined financial success, 2) are you measuring your projects against that definition, and 3) are you reporting the measurements to senior management? Give yourself an A if you do all three, a B if you do 1 and 2, and a C if you have done at least 1. If you failed the test, give yourself a C if any IT project in the organization has ever done all three.

Consider that you are making some personal financial investments. You have $6,000 to invest and you evaluate several opportunities. Your broker has offered you a great investment. You invest $500 per month for 12 months, and 12 months after the last investment the payout is $1,000 per month for 12 months. The risks are appropriate for this kind of return and you decide to do it. Your broker sets up a standing meeting every month to give you an update on your investment. For the first twelve months, you get a report that shows the time elapsed and percent of total investment made. The status of the investment is "green." After the complete investment you are assured that everything went as planned and the meetings cease. Twelve months later, you get a check for $250. Something went wrong, but based on the measurements your broker was using, you didn't know until it was too late. How many of your IT projects are measured in exactly the same way?

In most IT projects we measure time, budget, and milestones. However, these measures are almost never connected to delivered value or changes in risk, both of which are key components to the overall success of a project. In the investment example, let's assume that the investment was the purchase of mineral rights on some property. You expect to buy the rights over 12 months (perhaps on different pieces of property) and resell the rights two years later for twice what you paid for them. You assumed the properties you bought had a consistent likelihood of doubling in value; however, your project report simply told you that you spent money over time and got property. It did not measure expected future value of the property, so your broker bought property with more risk as others learned about the investment and property prices went up. During the intervening 12 months, your broker did not report on the expected returns, nor did he give you selling options to help manage the risks of the investment. He simply executed according to your instructions: Buy for $500 in month 1, sell in month 24. Because the sales price was $250, that's what you got. You measured time, invested money, and the number of properties purchased. Your return on investment was a mystery until you reach project payout. Does this sound familiar?

Too often we measure the wrong thing. Lest you fail by simply picking only positive things to measure, I must emphasize that effective measurement has three components:

- Meaningful measures
- Appropriate incentives
- Transparent use

Meaningful Measures

A software company, that shall remain nameless, measured the performance of its developers in lines of code written. What did it get? It got bloated software in which each module used many unnecessary lines of code. Everyone sees the fallacy in that now, but several arguably intelligent people thought it was a good idea at the time. The problem with this approach is that they chose a way of measuring the developers that had absolutely nothing to do with the delivered value and success of their projects.

Meaningful measures are connected to the business purpose of your project (chapter 5). I have been in innumerable project status meetings where progress is measured in weeks elapsed. If the project team does nothing for the first week of a ten-week project, is the project 10-percent done? Perhaps it is 0-percent done, or maybe even a negative 10-percent done. Try putting real investment numbers on your timeline. Say

> *I have been in innumerable project status meetings where progress is measured in weeks elapsed. If the project team does nothing for the first week of a ten-week project, is the project 10-percent done?*

you are making a $5MM investment in a project that will take one year and will deliver 5-percent productivity increases to your operation after being in place for a year. The project plan should indicate the burn rate of capital and assets — to include things like a productivity decrease while the system is implemented — and the expected rate of productivity increases during that first year of use. This should be compared with the projected period-by-period 5-percent increase.

In this case, the challenge for the project team is not just to spend according to plan and hit milestone targets, but to improve the rate of return. They can deliver ahead of time or under budget or provide greater productivity improvements. They should be able to see the effect on overall results when they miss a target as well as when they hit one early. If you indicate project status with green, yellow, and red (a common approach), a "green" project should show how many periods of productivity increases you are ahead of plan, or the ongoing increase in productivity percentage. I would call a project "yellow" that was poised to deliver only the productivity planned because even the slightest slip means you under deliver.

Treat your IT investment milestones more like a sales plan. The usual and customary commissions are paid for making plan, but the really juicy bonuses happen when you are ahead of plan. You need to stop measuring how many weeks you are into (or behind on) a project, and instead measure how much additional value the project team is providing above their promise. Remember it's not a schedule; it is a promise to return an investment.

At this point in a discussion, I am usually challenged on my example. Since when do IT projects have a clear investment estimate and a clear return?

At this point in a discussion, I am usually challenged on my example. Since when do IT projects have a clear investment estimate and a clear return? Aren't most projects a lot less definite? The answer is, of course, yes. However, this is part of the problem. If you don't ask for the same up-front measurement as you would for launching a product extension or building a new warehouse, you can't expect the risk profile of an IT project to be the same as other projects. A lack of discipline has caused the basic financial skills of most IT professionals to atrophy. You'll learn more about this when we discuss your team's fitness (chapter 9) and the problem of ignorance (chapter 10).

Delivered value over time works well when your costs and timelines are variable, but sometimes you can't move a milestone. If you purchase Electric Light Orchestra's Face the Music album on vinyl, at the beginning of the first track, you'll find a profound piece of poetry recorded backward: "The music is reversible, but time is not. Turn back. Turn back. Turn back." I've always found their delivery both fun and memorable, and their message particularly relevant to IT projects. If I may take liberty with their poetry, the point is you cannot add time to the calendar in order to hit a fixed mark in a slipped schedule. Sometimes you can work harder for short periods to make up for small slippages by using time that was set aside for things like sleep and your daughter's soccer game. However, if your hardware vendor delivers the hardware a week late, no amount of overtime will give you that week back. You simply cannot make the hardware arrive in the past. As ELO said, only the music is reversible.

This means that your project measurement must account for fixed cost and fixed calendar milestones. You must also connect delivered value to these fixed items. If your project delivers value at each month-end close and you slip one week, it only matters if the slippage causes you to miss a month-end close. If you don't miss a month-end close, you may have increased the risk of failure, and you may have increased variable costs by one week, but you have not decreased the delivered value. However, your one-week slip could cost one week of effort, but deny you one month of value if you miss a month-end close as a result.

Although the schedule might be a nightmare for project managers and feature prominently on their reports, the tasks-done-over-time aspect of the project is not the right thing to measure. Instead, your project manager should have a keen eye on fixed points in time, or durations that are not malleable that affect what the IT project delivers. For example, you can file your income taxes on time or you can pay a penalty. If a new IT system is going to give you the ability to file on time, but it isn't delivered early enough to actually allow you to file on time, you still pay the penalty. You want your measurements and project status meetings to highlight these items. If you add good risk management (chapter 8) a status meeting should go something like this:

> **Project Manager (PM):** "The file-on-time module will not be delivered in time for us to actually file

on time, putting us at risk of incurring a $100,000 penalty."

Executive Sponsor (EXEC): "The Street is not going to be happy if we take a tax filing penalty after all we have invested in this financial system. Why wasn't I informed about this earlier?"

PM: "Actually, you were. It was item number 14 on our risk matrix presented at the beginning of the project. Our avoidance plan was a pre-planned checkpoint with the tax group and the option to negotiate an extension.

"We did this last week and were granted an extension giving us the time we need to implement and file without the penalty being applied."

EXEC: "Will the slippage of the file-on-time module affect any other return-on-investment promises?"

PM: "Not in a negative way. But if you recall, we finished the way-cool-tax-slasher module early and by waiting to use the file-on-time module, this year we can apply $200,000 in additional tax benefit that was planned for next year."

EXEC: "Great, I'll make sure we mention that on the analyst call next week. Wall Street should be pretty happy that we are delivering value ahead of schedule even though it appears we are late on our tax filing."

This is the kind of conversation that results from measuring the right things.

When developing measurements, two common measures can be misleading. The first one is budget. "In budget" is almost always measured as expenditures over time. This measure is useless. I agree that the measure of how much of the planned investment has been consumed is critical. However, if that measure is not tied to delivered value, it doesn't matter how "in-budget" the project is; the numbers tell you nothing. Develop a habit of challenging budget numbers and tying the numbers to delivered value or forms of progress other than time.

> *"In budget" is almost always measured as expenditures over time. This measure is useless.*

Second, lines of code, pages of documentation, bugs found, and other measures of volume are equally useless in the context of time-passed and budget-spent. Just because a programmer developed a bunch of code, doesn't mean she did anything of value. Imagine you need a cabinet to store the dishes in a restaurant kitchen. You have 400 plates and 60 serving dishes and your carpenter reports to you that progress is going great. They've already built 17 cabinets. How big is a cabinet? How many plates can you store? What is progress really? Measuring the right things means measuring value delivered against the promise, and measuring the time needed to deliver that value.

Appropriate Incentives

Just measuring isn't enough. If the measurements mean nothing to those being measured they will be ignored. Worse, your team will "game" the system in order to achieve a meaningless measurement without actually achieving what you wanted to measure. During Operation Desert Shield (preceding Operation Desert Storm, the first Gulf war), I managed an intelligence processing and communications center. We were under a significant amount of stress, as you might imagine, and many of my team members had never done their jobs in a live environment. Wartime is the ultimate live environment because mistakes generally cost lives. Needless to say, tracking and managing performance of the team and the individuals was crucial. If we were to be effective in several weeks when the bullets started flying, I needed to know where to focus our efforts in training and process improvement.

I worked with my team leaders to develop a set of measures that would give us what we needed and we proceeded to track the team against those measures. We noticed that the night shift (we ran two twelve-hour shifts) consistently underperformed the day shift by just a little bit. Where we emphasized a measure, both teams improved but the night shift stayed just a little below the other team. Reviewing the details with the management team, we agreed that while the night shift had a slightly junior mix of people, they were perfectly capable of outperforming the day shift if they wanted to do so. They were satisfied to trail them as long as it wasn't by too much.

We had areas to work on, but overall the night shift behavior was not a great concern. They had a good sense of how far they could be from the day shift benchmark and it was an acceptable margin of difference. My desire, however, was to foster some internal competition to drive even better results. If the night shift raised the bar, the day shift would work to meet or beat it. As long as the night shift constantly trailed in performance only the day shift was responsible for improving the unit overall. My day shift leader suggested a specific competition. We agreed that his suggestion was fair and that the night shift team could win. If properly motivated, both teams would show us how well they could really perform. What was needed was sufficient incentive for the teams to truly compete. Each shift was asked to consider a one-week competition based on the rules we established, and to suggest an appropriate incentive that would motivate them to really compete.

I can't recall what the day shift asked for, but the competition moved in a new direction when the night shift leader announced their decision. I do not know how the thought entered their minds, but their incentive was both unexpected and brilliant. If they won the competition, their leader — in a public ceremony — would shave my head (that's right my head) and for the time it took to regrow my hair, I would serve as a visible symbol that the night shift was the winner. Considering the regular interaction I had with our senior leadership and other units, this was a way to get news of their victory the widest possible distribution. Everyone I met would ask about my change of hairstyle, and I would inevitably tell the story which would then be repeated by others. It was genius.

Before agreeing, I had a private conference with the day shift team. The day shift was competitive by nature. Their leader, after all, had suggested the competition. Most of my working hours were during the day shift and I considered that team mine as much as his. If I agreed to the terms of the night shift, they would work very hard to win. It was up to the day shift to prevent this from happening and causing embarrassment to a manager they considered their own. They assured me the night shift would not prevail. Remember the chapter on believing the hype (chapter 4)? I bought it hook, line, and sinker.

As you might have guessed, the day shift was every bit as interested in the head shaving as the night shift was. Without any significant increase in performance, the numbers simply flipped. The night shift was now performing the best and the day shift trailed by just a little bit. No amount of encouragement or threats would change the situation. The day shift made it appear as though they were working hard to outdo the night shift, but the final numbers told the real story. The only change was I was going to be bald for several weeks and have to tell the story of good measurements and bad incentives. I had a photo, conveniently lost before the publication of this book, which was the last remaining testament to the importance of matching incentives and measurements. If they never read this book, my children will never know.

This example of misguided incentives was a fairly low-cost lesson, but I have seen many projects, plagued by the effect of poor incentives, with much higher costs. In chapter 1, I introduced the concept of incentives for performance, discipline, and improvement. If you are going to follow that pattern, your overall goals, measurements, and incentives must be aligned. For example, remember Bill, my star overachiever? The timeframe in which he delivered was not the only measurement of his work. We tracked errors per delivered function point[8] to make sure our team was not sacrificing quality for speed. We also ran scheduled testing and code reviews, which meant I sometimes could not use a component that had been delivered early because it still needed a quality check. Our standard rule was that you did rework on your own time so, if you delivered poor quality, you had to fix it without getting any slack on your current scheduled deliverables. The incentive we paid in time given back to those who worked ahead of schedule was automatically reduced if they produced poor quality work. This worked well for a high-performing and quality-minded small organization. I would not be as relaxed with my measurements in other environments.

> *Measurement can be as much a disincentive as an incentive. The effectiveness of your measurements depends greatly on how they are used and the degree of transparency in their use.*

Transparent Use

Measurement can be as much a disincentive as an incentive. The effectiveness of your measurements depends greatly on how they are used and the degree of transparency in their use. If you are measuring the right thing and providing appropriate incentives, your measurements become truly powerful if they are openly shared. The project team shouldn't have to wait for the monthly project status review to know where they are. Even bad news needs to see the light of day as soon as possible (chapter 11).

It is important to note that I put transparency last on the list. This

[8] Jones, Capers. *Applied Software Measurement: Assuring Productivity and Quality.* New York: McGraw-Hill, 1996.

was intentional. Poor measures and ineffective incentives should not be combined with transparency. To start with, if your measures and incentives are just plain stupid, don't advertise the fact. If they are unfair, imbalanced or produce the wrong behavior, you are better off if the team does not start discovering who the blind followers are, who is manipulating the system, and who just doesn't care. When this comes out as a result of good measurement the team will either self-correct, or you may need to let some people find new opportunities. The latter option will usually be supported by the team. However, the self-correction as a result of making poor measurements transparent will probably cause you to lose some of your best team members.

After you have developed good measurements and incentives and have made those transparent, you can experiment with other measurements in the open with a greater degree of forgiveness when you make poor choices. I'm a huge fan of transparency, but use caution if this is new to your organization. It can be a help or a hindrance.

I once worked for a large organization that was broken into five operational groups. I was the technical lead for one of them. The largest group was half of the organization and had its own section chief. The other four, including mine, were grouped under another section chief. He was probably the most talented man I have ever worked for, and undoubtedly the most ruthless and driven. We were required to make special copies of all our daily work and place them in his in-box. Not only did we have to do our work to the organization's standards, we also built packets for him with painstaking detail so he could review absolutely everything his section had produced in a given day.

Every morning he had the exact same routine. He came in early, got his coffee, and sat at his desk in the center of the office reading. If you were lucky, he would make several notes on your packet and send it back for correction or sometimes a complete rework. Most often however he would shout in a commanding tone, "Caudill (or the name of whatever unlucky soul had triggered his wrath), what is this crap!?!" At this command, you were to drop whatever you were doing, scurry to his desk, and stand quietly while he told you in no uncertain terms that you were lower than a worm and your quality of work didn't befit a five-year-old. You were required to answer his questions meekly and without excuse then scurry back to your desk to correct the egregious errors he had found. The most frustrating part of this exercise was that he was always right. We became very good at our work.

We also became very good at moving our work through the system without him knowing about it. Some work was reviewed by other departments and might find its way to the infamous "hall of shame" where we displayed many stupid, but ultimately human, errors. These work products had to end up in his in-box because of the risk that someone else might single them out and he would notice they had not crossed his desk. But, some work stayed below the radar and we sent him only enough of those deliverables to keep him unsuspecting while we completed the rest without his knowledge.

At some point, his daily fun with his own section wasn't enough to satisfy him, and he decided we needed to compete with the other section to prove our superiority. From what he could tell, the size of each group was proportional to the output of the group. But, he wanted us to show we could do more with fewer resources. The other section was composed of one group and made up approximately half the organization. Our section was broken up in a similar fashion. The largest group was about half of our section. My group was about half of what remained, and the smallest group was about half of the next smallest group. Unfortunately for us, our section chief did not continue to measure our output based on what crossed his desk. He wanted a fair and open measure of the total organizational output, so he bullied one of the programmers to write a report that reached down into the governance system we used for releasing our work and he sent everyone a copy.

The new report gave him, and all of us, information nobody really wanted to see. Up until this point — except for the brutality of his daily work reviews — the organization was reasonably productive and the sections maintained good working relations. Most of the associates liked working there. My section chief's ill-advised transparency changed all that. First, he discovered that not everything had been making its way to his desk and, as he delved into the past, he found out how long it had been going on. My fellow group technical leads and I found ourselves in quite a bit of trouble. Next, he discovered that my team (about one-quarter the size of the largest group) was producing more output than anyone. Instead of praise, the two larger groups suddenly considered us the enemy and became aggressive competitors and antagonists because of the trouble this made for them. Last, the smallest group produced so little output, mostly due to its size, it barely registered on the report in comparison to everyone else. This team was accused of being asleep at the wheel.

Through some very serious behind-the-scenes politics, all the group technical leads worked together to eventually cause the report to become permanently unavailable. We found alternative ways to produce measures that satisfied our section chief, who knew he had been foolish but was not about to admit it. It took us several months to bring productivity back to a reasonable level — it had plummeted during the crisis of transparency. One of the smaller sections never recovered and eventually everyone in it transferred out to other positions. It remained unmanned until the section chief was promoted to another position.

> *Heroes and those who support hero syndrome can use partial transparency as a means to perpetuate the syndrome.*

Like this example of complete transparency gone awry, heroes and those who support hero syndrome can use partial transparency as a means to perpetuate the syndrome. Heroes always want to look good. They will actively support timesheets, overtime reports, number of tasks accomplished and other measures of overwork.

When these measures are used alone, the heroes look really good and everyone else is ranked as only human. However, if you remove the effect of extra effort by showing productivity per hour, or minutes per task, you might find your heroes less productive than your mere mortals.

Transparency is not always bad. I recently visited a call center for telesales, customer support, etc. As you might imagine, they measure many different things from call statistics to order completeness to customer satisfaction. The reporting team produces daily numbers (some of them in real-time) on an easy-to-access website where everyone can see how both the organization and individuals are doing. Everything is in the open. If you as an individual are underperforming on a consistent basis, it is no surprise to anyone when you are fired. In the same way, everyone knows which team will win the monthly competition on a particular statistic. The management team constantly evaluates the measures against the goals of the organization to ensure they are measuring what they want to get. They also regularly reevaluate the incentives to make sure they are getting what they measure.

I was struck by the positive work environment. I sat with many of the operators to get a feel for their work. Everyone I met was positive and enjoyed work that I would personally consider mind-numbing. Much of the positive attitude had to do with the measurements. Everyone could see the difference they made in the organization. Comparisons of telephone sales and service versus direct sales and service were always available and this team took its job seriously. It was important to them that a customer served over the phone was even more satisfied than one who got face-to-face service. In addition to basic efficiency measures, the group could see cost-to-serve measurements. Telephone is not always the cheapest way to serve a customer and the group tracked customers being moved into and out of telephone service. Every team member could look at their individual and team numbers and see what they had contributed to the company that day. Combining good measurements with complete transparency made this organization both high-performing as well as a great place to work.

Tackling Measurement

Measuring the right things is tricky. It takes practice. This is one area where unlike school, life gives us the test first and the lesson afterward. Russ and I use three tools, with varying degrees of success, to guide ourselves toward effective measurement. These are: benefits over time, architectural milestones, and success metrics. None of these tools is a guarantee of success by itself, but each helps in its own way to prevent errors. You should map each of these tools against your business purpose (chapter 5) to ensure consistency and then develop your measurements to match.

Tool: Benefits over Time

As I've mentioned several times in this chapter, some of the benefits of your IT project are variable and some are fixed. You need to capture both and anchor each in the context of time. Russ and I generally produce this as a list of benefits and the conditions surrounding them. The key questions this list should answer are "why" and "when." Why are you doing this IT project? What are the resulting benefits? What is the delivered value for your IT investment broken into individual elements? When do you get those benefits? What time must elapse? What is the duration of the benefit? What particular calendar events affect the benefit? These are the questions you must answer as briefly and directly as possible.

For example, pretend I am building the U-catchem sales system, which will support back-end proposal and contract creation for our sales force. Here are the benefits:

• Reduction in headcount: Three fewer temporary workers hired at each month-end close, for a total reduction of 36 hours of contract work per month, as illustrated in figure 1.

Benefit	When	Conditions	Opportunity	Measurement
Reduce temp headcount by 1 person	March	50% of the sales force must be on the system prior to March 28th. Fewer than 50% provides no value. More than 50% provides no more value (except as below). Missing the deadline moves the value back one month.	If the full 50% of the sales force can be brought online by 24 hours prior to any month-end close the benefit starts that month.	1. total # of salesmen (baseline) 2. # of salesmen on the system 3. time it takes to get a salesman on the system 4. # of salesmen who can be brought on concurrently
Reduce temp headcount by 2 people	June	95% of the sales force must be on the system prior to June 26th. Fewer than 95% provides no value. More than 95% provides no more value (except as below). Missing the deadline moves the value back one month.	If the full 95% of the sales force can be brought online by 24 hours prior to any month-end close the benefit starts that month.	Same as above
Reduce temp headcount by 3 people	July	100% of the sales force must be on the system prior to July 30th. Fewer than 100% provides no value. Missing the deadline moves the value back one month.	If the full 100% of the sales force can be brought online by 24 hours prior to any month-end close the benefit starts that month.	Same as above

Figure 1: Benefits-over-time example 1

- Reduction in the number of overnight mail packages by an average of four per customer contract.
- Reduction in printed materials sufficient to remove two of the three leased print/copy machines at the sales support center.
- Reduction in non-pay activity for the sales force sufficient for a 2- to 5-percent increase in total customer contracts.

These benefits were included in the business purpose (chapter 5), and the project was approved based on the value of all of these benefits. When the project was proposed, some assumptions were made about how long it would take to develop and implement, resulting in an estimated time when the benefits would begin. However, these benefits have not yet been set into a context of time. This gives the project team an opportunity to look into how to optimize the project for maximum benefit, where to look for problems in failing to deliver against time-bound benefits, and what to measure to stay on track.

To convert these benefits into benefits over time, the team has to do a little more investigation. When looking at the first benefit, the team finds that the month-end close work is based on the number of salesmen regardless of how many customers and contracts they have. It is also clear that the work is not directly proportional to the number of salesmen. Until 50 percent of the sales force is on the system, all three temps will be needed. After that, two temps will be needed, until 95 percent of the sales force is on the system. Since the month-end close activity is based on the previous month's contracts, as soon as a salesman is on the system (those on 24 hours prior to month-end close) the benefits are realized. Thus, if fewer than 50 percent of the salesmen are on the system the day before a month-end close, no benefit is realized.

The team researches the customer contracts and finds that each salesman handles a different number of contracts. Contracts take four weeks to complete. The distribution of contracts initiated each week is sufficiently even so they can predict that a salesman

Benefit	When	Conditions	Opportunity	Measurement
Eliminate an average of 4 overnight mail charges per customer contract	Four weeks after each salesman goes live	A contract takes 4 weeks to process. Average weekly contracts * 4 = ongoing reduction in weekly overnight mail starting no later than 4 weeks from the salesman going live (some benefit may accrue earlier)	Add salesmen based on their average weekly number of contracts in order from largest to smallest to front-load the benefits.	1. # of weekly contracts per salesman 2. average # of overnight packages sent weekly prior to the system going live (baseline)

Figure 2: Benefits-over-time example 2

new to the system will convert one-quarter of his contracts each week until he is fully automated. This information results in the benefits-over-time chart above.

I won't detail the other benefits, but you should have an idea of what might be on the chart. If the opportunity for more contracts differs by salesman, you will want to organize them by those who promise the greatest additional revenue. This will have to be reconciled with benefit #2, which suggests you organize them by average weekly contracts. Some juggling may be required to optimize your benefits, but you could significantly change the first year's return if you connect the benefits relationship to time and develop ways to recognize the greatest benefits as early as possible.

Also note the measures you will need not only to measure the benefit, but to determine a baseline (where needed) and to monitor the delivery. Evaluating the benefits and time relationship early in the project will allow you to find critical measurements before you need them.

Tool: Architectural Milestones

Once you have a benefits-over-time list, your project manager, IT architect and engineers need to work together to determine what project milestones you need to hit in order to drive the benefits. Do not be satisfied with milestones that show volume of work completed or budget expended. Your project milestones should be directly related to business benefit. I have worked on very large projects (that were not under my control) where features and enhancements were rolled up into scheduled releases, which in themselves were large projects. Most often in major new modules or fresh installations, the benefit-to-milestone relationship is clear. Rarely, for modifications to existing implementations, do I see any connection between feature/function change and business benefit.

I wonder sometimes if a particular change is only to relieve the annoyance or frustration of one person, or if an entire workforce will gain a significant productivity advantage. If it isn't obvious, we categorize the change in a mystery category with an unclear urgency and have no idea that if we had only delivered request #245 a day sooner, the finance department could have let a $50,000 contract lapse. Instead, that contract has now been renewed for six months.

Architectural milestones are a way to connect systems work with delivered value. You can build this into your project plan using your favorite Gantt charting tool. Follow these basic steps:

1. Chart the implementation in context with related business activities and milestones.

2. Generalize the timeline and task breakdown.

3. Extend the timeline to include use of the new system until all benefits are realized.

4. Identify key milestones and the corresponding benefits.

At first glance, the example in Figure 3 on the next page looks like a regular Gantt chart from a typical project plan. However, if you look more closely, the task and milestone descriptions are a bit unusual. For example, "Demonstrate leading-edge technology"

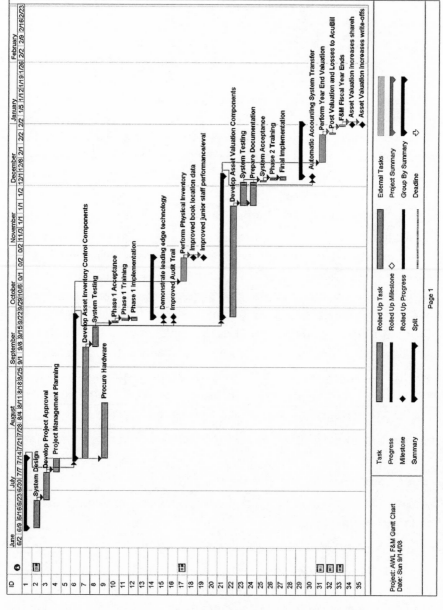

Figure 3: Architectural milestones example

doesn't mean giving a demo of the system. It is actually a delivered value. The business that made an IT investment in this project has a problem: They recruit hot young lawyers straight out of the best schools and those recruits are increasingly concerned about the availability of technology to aid them in their work. This particular firm is lagging behind. One of their hopes for this new system is that it will demonstrate the practical implementation of some cutting-edge technology to improve recruitment. Using this plan, recruiters can know when they will be able to talk about and demonstrate how "up-to-date" the firm is.

Note also task #31. This is an end-of-year valuation of assets (the IT system manages some of the firm's assets). The asset valuation will occur whether the IT system is ready or not. Thus, the time-bound aspect of valuation is firmly in the plan. Should the project slip, the business value delivered around the asset valuation process might be lost.

By putting a twist into your usual and customary Gantt chart by connecting tasks and value, you build a foundation on which to have relevant and useful conversations about project progress. In addition, you set up a constant reminder to anyone exploring your project's progress of why you made the IT investment in the first place. Posting this kind of a chart in a common area or on a project website allows team members, management, and the eventual users of the system to see how your IT team's work results in real business value.

Tool: Success Metrics

Now that you have evaluated the relationship between benefits and time and have developed your project plan around those benefits, you need a way to communicate where you are in a way easy to digest by those not intimately familiar with the measurements. Our favorite tool is the success metrics dashboard. I have seen many project review templates and project status dashboards, but most of these are based on the usual and customary metrics of time, budget, and volume of deliverables. Using your architectural milestones, you can build a dashboard that focuses on delivered value.

The format of your success metrics dashboard is not terribly important; content has trumped format in every case we have encountered. Regardless of how accustomed your executive or project team is to glossy printouts or colorful presentations, a solid representation of value-based milestones will get their attention. We use a simple table in a document showing the project tasks and milestones that are either necessary precursors to delivering value (usually steps on the critical path), high-risk items (chapter 8), or directly related to delivering value. Russ likes to use colors (green,

U-catchem project Success Metrics Dashboard as of July				
	date	measure	value	measurement
Design/Blueprint				
business purpose	July	document approved	pass	pass/fail
benefits over time	July	document approved	pass	pass/fail
architectural milestones	July	Gantt chart approved	pass	pass/fail
system design	August	design submitted for test		pass/fail
design acceptance test	August	revised design tested and accepted		pass/fail
project review stage gate	September	review of investment vs. return		pass/fail
Development				
contract mgr module test	October	module test plan passed		pass/fail
month-end module test	October	module test plan passed		pass/fail
integration test	November	integration test plan passed		pass/fail

conversion test	November	conversion test plan passed		pass/fail
training plan complete	December	training materials & plan approved		pass/fail

Implementation

baseline measurement	November	baseline measurements taken	35%	weighted value of completions (of 100%)
system installation	December	installed system functional test		pass/fail
production data load & test	December	customer & integration data loaded and tested		pass/fail
salesman training begins	December	salesmen trained	0 / 236	trained / total
conversion of salesmen	January	salesmen converted to new system	0 / 236	converted / total

End Game

temp headcount reduction	begins March	reduction of 36 contractor hours/month	0	contractor hours
reduce overnight packages	begins March	total $ from $75M baseline	0	dollars saved (baseline - actual)
printer/copier retirement	begins February	incremental reduction of two machines	0	machines retired
increase in contracts	begins in May	increase from 10M contracts of between 2-5%	0	actual weekly contracts in new system - baseline weekly average contracts of converted salesmen
increase in projected revenue	begins in May	based on contract increase. Not all increases will be attributed to this project as the business is also focused on increasing revenue per contract which is unrelated to this project.	0	Contract dollar YTD vs. prior YTD

Figure 4: Success metrics dashboard example

yellow, red) to indicate status, and I like to add value and measurement data.

We call this the success metrics dashboard because it should be completely focused on what it takes to declare success. Any delivered value that is unnecessary for success should be noted, but downplayed. This is not to prevent you from delivering it, but to ensure that the focus is on what must be done. Additional delivered value will reflect well on the project only if the necessary goals are achieved. Don't be so distracted by small victories that you lose sight of the goal.

Using the example of the U-catchem system I described earlier, a success metrics dashboard might look something like the chart in Figure 4. You might want to be a little more specific with your dates, but this should give you an idea of how to format your dashboard. Our recommendation is to keep it to one page (or one screen if you do it online) and make it available to everyone at all times. Don't wait for a project review meeting or some formal presentation. Every time the status of a success metric changes, post an update so everyone who cares about the project can see it.

Chapter 8: Hope as a Risk-Management Strategy

R isk management is one of our favorite topics. You could say this book is primarily about risk management, and risk management most certainly forms a large part of the content in the seminars we give. Recently we were giving a full-day seminar for a room of about seventy attendees. We arrived the afternoon before and Russ began a routine that is part of our standard risk management.

We have worked with this particular conference organizer for many years and the people who manage the details are quite familiar with our "routine." It is often fodder for friendly joking. Russ has a detailed plan and works according to a schedule, checklist, etc. I am a bit more of a free spirit and appear to be completely unconcerned about the following day's sessions. A long standing joke revolves around the time that I didn't show up and was awakened by a phone call ten minutes before the session began. Exactly on time, I swaggered into the room, strapped on my lavaliere microphone and started the session.

Despite the joking and our different styles, we both have developed a pattern of good risk management accompanying our speaking engagements. For this particular session the organizers had run a week-long conference with a short staff and had done extremely well. We were providing a post-conference session that was an add-on to the main event and the team was exhausted from their week. Since we are regulars, they were confident that our session would go well and they were starting to relax. When we arrived, they immediately started joking about Russ' "routine" and suggested we just wait until the morning to do our final checks. Some good natured banter circled the room, but Russ insisted that his risk-management plan called for certain things to be done now and he proceeded to do them.

The session materials are a little bit tricky as we have the typical session notebook, some individual handouts for our workshop exercises, and a packet with the final answers to be distributed at the end of the session. This group had never failed to deliver the materials as expected. Nevertheless, Russ methodically examined every piece ensuring we had everything and sufficient copies of each item. His risk-management plan called for us to confirm the materials early enough that we could print any shortfalls at a local business center or copy shop that evening if necessary. I joined in the joking, but was sure not to stand in the way of Russ' work. I can appear to be caviler because I trust his risk-management plan. This time, however, something was missing. The main seminar handouts were not with the other materials.

Shari, who is an excellent conference organizer and was instigator of most of the teasing, quickly made a call. Yes, the materials had been printed and shipped and she had the tracking numbers. Russ continued his methodical checks and I accompanied Shari to the conference center receiving area. They tracked the packages to the local warehouse, but they were not set to be delivered until the next day. We discovered later that they had been mistakenly shipped with the wrong priority. Unfortunately, the warehouse had not sorted the packages — that would happen overnight. Thus, we could not send a courier to pick up the boxes until the following morning. This would be too late as the materials would be needed by at least some attendees from the start.

After gathering information about how we might get the packages and our options for printing the materials, I returned to Russ to discuss the options. They were:

1. Arrive at 6:00 a.m. at the package warehouse where we would meet the manager and hopefully find the package. Drive the one-hour trip back to the conference center and distribute the materials at the last minute. This would cost someone several hours of early morning driving and would force several people to come to work early to accommodate our needs. One of these was the warehouse manager so we incurred an additional risk related to the warehouse manager, whom we did not know personally, arriving on time.

2. Consider the printing and shipping a loss, and reprint the materials at a local shop. We would need to rush to ensure we got the job materials there and checked so they would have enough time to run the job before closing for the night. This would also be at considerable expense.

3. Print a basic black-and-white, stapled copy of the materials for use by those who are note-takers (estimating 40 percent of the group). We would distribute these limited copies along with an explanation about practical risk management at the beginning of the session and then distribute the nice copies of the materials after they arrived later in the morning. The in-house business center could process the job before dinner.

Russ asked a few clarifying questions and we discussed the budget with Shari. He was quickly able to decide. We would take option #3 and if that was a little embarrassing the people hurt most were us rather than our attendees. We opened the session with a discussion of this event and practical risk management. Later one of the attendees accused us of making the whole thing up as a bit of theatrics to improve the session. I wish that had been true.

Something the risk-management plan called for was my availability. One of the reasons I can be relaxed and cavalier about the pre-seminar work is that I am the slack in the project plan. I am the resource "on the bench." Once the risk occurred, I walked the length and breath of the conference center getting pricing, being firm with couriers, gathering facts, and developing options. Russ could continue his work knowing that I was taking care of the "emergency" and that I would return with reasonable options. Our risk-management plan considered all of this and, what could have been a minor disaster turned into a learning opportunity.

Sometimes, however, even a good risk plan can lean toward heroism as the risk mitigation technique. You have to constantly check your plan for signs of hero syndrome and, when faced with mitigation options, select those that solve the problem even when they do not put the spotlight on a hero. We could have chosen to take the early morning trip to the package warehouse and let everyone know how early we started our day.

> *Sometimes even a good risk plan can lean toward heroism as the risk mitigation technique. You have to constantly check your plan for signs of hero syndrome and, when faced with mitigation options, select those that solve the problem even when they do not put the spotlight on a hero.*

The wild ride returning just in time to deliver the materials would make good folklore, but would be bad risk management. The path of heroism included too many risks itself. We could get stuck in traffic and not only the materials, but also the presenters would be missing when the workshop started. We could have made the trip and still not returned with the materials if the warehouse manager was late or the package could not be found. Even in a successful scenario, we would begin our workshop already tired and stressed from the early morning adventure. Risk management alone will not eliminate hero syndrome; you have to practice managing risk well.

Planning for the Unknown

From my observations inside IT organizations, we're pretty good at issue tracking, bug tracking, status tracking, problem tracking, request tracking, and many other forms of it-already-happened tracking. But what about I-hope-this-doesn't-happen tracking? When we face an uncertain capital investment market, we manage risk by developing a hedge or purchasing options. These techniques are activities that help us reduce the impact of uncertainty.

In IT, risk management is about tracking what hasn't happened yet and making concrete plans around what to do about the potential event. This might include preventing it from happening or causing it to happen at a non-critical juncture. If it does happen, the risk-management plan dictates how to respond. If you don't have basic risk-management practices operating in your IT department or if you don't have a risk-management strategy for your high-risk IT projects (which is all of them), then you are managing your investments unwisely.

If you think you do manage your risks, let me see if I can't convince you otherwise. In only a very few IT projects have I seen consistent and adequate risk management. Consider the two groups at the conference I described earlier: the speakers and the organizers. The speakers had a written plan for managing risks and executed the plan methodically. The organizers have done this so many times that risk management is built into their practices; however, this time they were understaffed and some of the best practices weren't practiced. Thus a small item slipped through causing them to scramble much later than was necessary.

If you think you are doing risk management, you should be able to put this book down, and quickly (as in one minute or less) be holding a printed copy of a risk-management plan that shows the top risks, their likelihood and impact as evaluated recently, and an avoidance or mitigation plan. This plan should also be in the hands of anyone who is part of the avoidance or mitigation plan so they have clear instructions if a risk becomes an issue (meaning it occurs). If you cannot do this, you are not managing IT risks adequately.

> **It is important to understand that identifying and even tracking risks is not the same as managing risks.**

It is important to understand that identifying and even tracking risks is not the same as managing risks. Although it is helpful to know what might happen and to note when it happens, what you really want to do is change the outcome. Good risk managers are able to deliver value despite the risks and not just because they get lucky. When the bulk of your risks are adequately managed, it is surprising how often you "get lucky" because you are not fighting predictable fires; instead, you are handling actual emergencies.

Data Center Move

Russ writes: This story comes from my recent experience with a mid-size (350 employees) company (hereinafter, "the firm"). I spent the better part of a year there, officially as a project manager, but unofficially filling gaps in the IT department, doing everything from process engineering, workload analysis/reporting, compliance monitoring, and even documentation.

The firm had decided to move its main office from the city to the suburbs and I was asked to be the project manager of the IT aspects of the move. In reality, I was co-managing it with the Chief Technology Officer (CTO). The project was quite simply this: Shut down all the IT equipment (workstations, servers, and anything else that was either connected to or even vaguely resembled a computer) on Friday, move it to Maryland, and have it back up and running by Monday. The firm had an in-house IT staff, long-term contractors, and an outside company ("the Experts") who were brought in specifically to pack the equipment, move it, unpack it, and set it up again.

Seeing that the needed resources and physical moving of all the equipment had been pretty much addressed, I focused on laying out the schedule. From then on, I knew what would be the biggest challenge: managing the risks. Anyone who has ever handled a move that required more than a couple of buddies and a pickup truck knows there are about a gazillion things that can go wrong, and that it often takes weeks to get all the details sorted out. We didn't have weeks; we had two days and three nights to work out most of them. The only way we could be successful was to anticipate what could go wrong and prepare in advance to handle the problems.

The first thing I did was build a risk matrix. I created a list of all the things that might go wrong, ranked each on both the likelihood of it happening and the impact of it happening, and described how we would either deal with it if it happened, or what we could do to prevent it from happening at all. I got together with the IT folks and brainstormed, coming up with a list of about 30 items — everything from the obvious and reasonable to the seemingly ridiculous. Here are some examples:

- Workstation(s) fail to reboot
- Critical equipment is lost in transit
- Server is damaged and does not restart
- Infrastructure problems in new site (e.g., failure of power, Internet, network, etc.)
- Hurricane/severe weather during the move
- Moving van in severe accident, all contents destroyed

After we listed all the things we could think of, we ranked them *based on likelihood and impact and sorted them from highest rank (i.e., most likely and/or most severe) to lowest. We then went through another round of brainstorming to determine how we would mitigate and/or prevent each potential risk.*

It was important to keep in mind that time was the most valuable asset we would have during the move. Two and a half days isn't much time, no matter how many people you have. Anything we could do in the weeks prior would pay off tenfold during crunch time. After I built the risk matrix, I pulled out all the tasks we could do ahead of time and put them in the project as advance tasks. Here are some of the items we came up with to mitigate or prevent the risks:

- *Perform extensive testing at new site to confirm infrastructure functionality.*

- *Confirm the restart process for each server is already documented, and update if necessary.*

- *Confirm back-up schedule, validate backup before shutting down on Friday.*

- *Perform a physical inventory of all IT equipment.*

- *Perform a physical inventory of in-stock parts and critical spares.*

- *Review and update vendor support information. Contact critical vendors in advance to confirm weekend support availability. Pay extra to ensure availability if necessary.*

- *Confirm hot-site server functionality.*

- *Develop a plan to test each workstation after set up.*

- *Have the help desk team plan to set up the new help desk area for triage/repair for workstations and have them move tools and a small collection of spare parts themselves so they would not have to hunt for them.*

- *Develop a test plan that includes each server, to be executed Sunday. This plan should include a printed test plan, printed validation checklist and printed "trouble ticket" forms since the automated IT support systems would probably be unavailable.*

- *Rank servers by priority and schedule startup and testing accordingly.*

- *Survey loading dock area at both locations to see if heavy rain would be a problem*

- *Ask the Experts to guarantee weather-tightness of all moving vehicles.*

- *Have the CTO transport the backup media personally, so that a vehicle mishap could only destroy either servers or backups, but not both.*

What we would do if we ran into any of these problems at the new site?

- *Prioritize the diagnoses/repair work based on the server rank.*

- *Fix it! Execute normal resolution procedures in the new help desk area.*

- *Make a go/no-go decision by 6:00 p.m. Sunday to commit to having each server up, or switch to the hot-site version.*

- *Switch that server's functionality to the hot-site as needed.*

The weekend of the move came and, of course, things didn't go as smoothly as we had hoped they would. Having both me and the CTO as project managers ended up working fantastically (it could've been a disaster). I managed things at the old site and he managed the new site.

We got underway Friday evening, and it quickly became apparent that the Experts had grossly underestimated how much equipment we had to pack and move. It took hours to remove all the equipments from the racks and pack it up. The new space contained all new racks and would be completely re-cabled, since the old data center cabling had devolved into a chaotic mass of untraceable cables. Additionally, the lease agreement for the existing space required us to completely empty the old data center. So, after the equipment was removed, with wire cutters in hand we cut and yanked fistfuls of multi-colored spaghetti cable and trashed it, not realizing how this would affect us later.

In addition to the Experts' under-estimation of the equipment we had to move, nobody had considered the fact that the Experts had brought in their own separate moving company, meaning we would have two moving companies trying to simultaneously use the one available freight elevator. It was a huge relief to get both moving company foremen together and see them agree to "play nice" with each other and take turns.

The moving van accident taken with my cell phone camera — Our moving truck wasn't just caught in the traffic jam, it was *the cause* of the traffic jam.

Around 10:00 p.m., things got really interesting. That's when the Experts told us their movers would be leaving at midnight, even though they were far from finished. Worse, he told us they might not be able to get them back to finish Saturday since they were already booked!!

We still had carts and carts of hardware that hadn't been moved yet!! We wracked our brains and then the light went on. I tracked down the foreman of the other moving company, the ones moving all the non-IT stuff ... could they handle the extra load? He thought for a second, looked at the hallway jammed with a mix of the two moving company's carts *and said, "Yeah, we can take theirs too." I wanted to hug him!*

I paused for a minute after he walked away, then spent the next half hour rearranging the carts in the hallway so all the ones with computer equipment were closest to the freight elevator doors.

As things wound down for night, it was time for me to head to the new site. I walked out and around the block the get my car. I looked at all the traffic and shook my head at the fact that, even at 11:30 at night, city traffic was still bumper-to-bumper. Oh wait no, it's because there's an accident at the intersection. Even one of our moving trucks is caught in the jam. At least he's toward the front of the backup, close to where the accident must be, so hopefully they'll let him by soon. Oh no, he is the accident scene.

Thankfully, the damage was only minor, and the truck was return-ing to the old site and was therefore empty. Disaster narrowly avoided!

I got to the new site, and things were frantic, but productive. Our folks were helping the Experts search for and unpack what they could find and getting some of the equipment in place. Saturday would be the big day for assembling and breathing life into the new data center. We turned the lights off around 3:00 a.m.

Back at work at 8:00 a.m., the Experts arrived to begin their work. They asked the CTO if he knew where the reel of new Ethernet cable was so they could start cutting it. "New cable??" he replied. "You guys are supposed be supply the cable!" We desperately began searching for someplace where we could purchase a mile and half of CAT 6 Ethernet cable … on a Saturday. We made several calls, but nobody with anywhere near that quantity was open. Exactly who was at fault became completely irrelevant as we realized we were facing a very real possibility of utter failure. They considered re-using some of the old cable until I described in gory detail how we had gone about extracting it from the old data center.

The CTO thought some more, then considered the fact that the new phone system was wired with the same kind of cable, and maybe the contractor had some left over. He called, and the contractor said, "Yeah I got about 7,500 feet left over downstairs, how much do you need?" All I can say is, sometimes it is better to be lucky than good.

That turned out to be the last of our major disasters. Although we lost several hours of precious time, all of our risk mitigation steps paid off. Here are some of the other events from that weekend:

- *Several servers did fail to restart. However, we quickly triaged these and used critical-spares to replace whatever component had not survived the move. Thankfully, none required data restoration, but we could've done this if necessary.*

- *Every server's functionality was tested on Sunday morning per our plan. One of the core systems servers restarted successfully Saturday, but the application failed to respond during testing. We engaged the vendor's tech support team, which had been informed about the move in advance, and spent several hours with them successfully fixing the problem.*

- *Uninterruptable power supply for the most critical computer went missing for several hours, but was finally located in a corner of the old site, packed but thus-far overlooked by the movers. We got it on the next truck. Had we been unable to find it, we were prepared to switch appropriate operations to the hot-site.*

- *Many keyboards, mice, and monitors were unevenly distributed so we came up short in some areas. But, we had purchased extras of each before the move so we didn't have to waste time looking for the misplaced ones. All of them did eventually turn up.*

- *Several workstations suffered hardware failures, but our test process discovered many of these before Monday, when the general staff arrived. Additionally we had the tools and parts needed to fix them readily available, so almost all of them were taken care of before Monday morning.*

- *Yes, we had users with lots of issues on Monday, but one of the mitigations in the weeks before was to hire temps to augment the help desk for the first week. Additionally, just about every other IT staff member (including me and the CTO) helped to close help desk tickets.*

Steve called me Sunday afternoon to ask how it was going. After I told him about all of the problems we had (and sent him a picture of the accident scene), he asked me, "Geez, are you guys going to make your deadline?"

"Of course," I replied, completely serious. "Why wouldn't we?" Everything else that went wrong went wrong exactly according to plan, so we were still on schedule.

Sunday night, at about 6:00 p.m., we assessed the status. Every critical server was up, running, and functioning as necessary. We had one Dev/QA box that was still down, but that could be addressed in a non-critical manner. Almost all the workstations had been tested and, although some were still down, we at least knew they needed to be fixed. The go/no-go decision was made: No operation would need to be moved to the hot-site. We had done it, and a brief celebration followed.

This was one of the most intense yet rewarding projects I have ever worked on. Although we lost hours to risks that we had failed to anticipate, we made up the time by being prepared for the risks we had anticipated, and that was what made the difference between failure and success.

Things Go Wrong — According to Plan

Russ is a careful and experienced risk manager — a skill that takes considerable practice. Without his experience you can still spot risk plans that are unworkable and projects that don't really have a plan. It all comes down to a simple rule: The 70-hour work week is not risk mitigation. If your IT people never seem to go home, somebody is mitigating risks using brute force and your team is suffering from a case of hero syndrome. For obvious reasons, this is a bad idea.

Your project team might remind you that Murphy's Law is, "If it can go wrong, it will." Simply tell them that Murphy can be managed.

If you want your IT projects to succeed, ask for a list of risks and a management plan. You don't necessarily have to understand all the gory details; however, the impossible is often easy to spot. Run the list by one of the team who always seems to be working late and ask if they plan to go home on time. Hysterical laughter is usually a sign that the risk-management plan is unreasonable.

Your project team might remind you that Murphy's Law is, "If it can go wrong, it will." Simply tell them that Murphy can be managed. Unless your project manager is a complete novice — in which case you have a different problem (chapter 6) — they will know from hard experience what can go wrong on an IT project. Get a few veterans in a room and brainstorm a list of risks. You'll find things like: Module X won't handle our data volumes and vendor Y won't deliver the equipment on time.

Tool: Risk Matrix

Figure 5 shows a risk matrix like the one Russ described. Give each risk a likelihood score from 1-5 where 1 is unlikely to happen and 5 is a sure thing. Do the same with impact where 1 means it has little effect on the project and 5 means it's a show-stopper. Multiply those numbers to get a risk score. We use 1-5 because 1-3 is too general and more than 5 is too granular. The multiplied score helps balance high-likelihood/low-impact and low-likelihood/high-impact risks. When you have your scores, sort the list from largest score to smallest.

Risk	Likelihood	Impact	Score	Mitigation
Hardware not available on time	5	4	20	Request delivery guarantees when ordering equipment
Key project sponsor leaves company	3	5	15	Identify most likely success or determine project stance
Proposed technology does not work	2	4	8	Identify back-up technology/schedule

Figure 5: Risk matrix example

Now you have a quick-and-dirty list of risks by importance (meaning the one most important to manage is at the top). This is a 30- to 60-minute exercise on most IT projects (even huge ones). Pick the top risks and ask your team to bring back a management plan. They should avoid, mitigate, and/or front-load each of the risks in a reasonable manner:

- Avoiding risks means developing a plan that takes a path that negates the risk altogether. For example if vendor A is having quality problems, switch to vendor B whose quality inspires confidence.

- Mitigating risks means developing a plan to manage the outcome after the risk occurs, like Russ did with his data center move.

- Front-loading risks means moving risks forward in the project so, if they occur, they have a negligible impact. If you think your hardware vendor may not deliver on time, ask them to deliver earlier than you need the hardware. Then, nobody cares if they are late.

All these management steps will cost you something, but this is no different than risk management for any other type of investment. Buying a hedge still means you make a financial commitment. Purchasing an option costs you something even while it reduces your risks.

Chapter 9: Round Is a Shape (Not Keeping Fit)

One of my favorite comic characters is the cat Garfield. The cynical, irreverent, and seriously overweight cat when encouraged to get in shape responds, "Round is a shape!" I recently watched an interview with a popular actor who described what makes an actor great. He recalled that in the 1920s and 30s, greatness was all about glamour. In the 40s and 50s, greatness was strength. Then method acting became critical and the measure of greatness was the ability to create a very personal moment on camera. Now, he jested, great actors are physically fit[9].

I've lived through the North American fitness fetish from the granola eaters of the 1970s to the very strange exercise outfits of the 1980s to home fitness machines to the rise of everything organic and "heart healthy." I'm all for fitness, but most of the people I know who were (or are) enamored with fitness fads are, in the long run, every bit as out of shape as the average American couch potato.

As you probably know and, no doubt, your doctor reminds you, better diet and exercise are the almost universal cures to much of what ails us physically. Yet despite the aforementioned health crazes, we spend our time in a conference room, cubicle, or parked in front of the TV eating yesterday's cold, take-out pizza. Of course, if you

[9] "Alec Baldwin." *Inside the Actors Studio.* Season 13, Episode 1309: *The Actors Studio,* October 22, 2007.

are an up-and-coming executive in a large company, you are probably in reasonably good physical condition because these companies have stopped hiring executives who are at risk of a major health crisis. It's easy to tell which ones are which. Many of our personal habits (particularly the bad ones) are hidden from plain sight. People have to get to know us to know if we are addicted to news channels or video games or if we mistreat our pets. Our physical condition, however, is tough to hide.

IT Fitness

IT endeavors require mental skills and, as with physical skills, you have to exercise to stay in shape. But how can you tell? The IT associate who doesn't have a balanced mental diet and exercise in his field looks very much like the one who does. When selecting the right people (chapter 6), how can you tell who is really on top of their game? If you are stuck with a somewhat out-of-shape team, what should you do about it? After all, a little pudginess around the middle doesn't mean the team can't handle the project, right?

When was the last time your team had a workout? Not a physical workout, but some basic IT or business skills work — mental gymnastics.

Wrong. When your IT group is out of shape, you can't tell what they can do. Maybe they can handle your project and maybe not. Without the regular benchmark of conditioning you have no measure of their actual capability. When was the last time your team had a workout? Not a physical workout, but some basic IT or business skills work — mental gymnastics. IT skills atrophy just as our muscles do. Your IT budget and schedule should both allow and encourage regular basic skill building.

One of the practices I like to institute with my teams is a weekly brown-bag study group. Choose a good business or IT book and discuss a chapter a week. Get a good facilitator who will challenge the team to not just skim but read and thoughtfully consider the material. Certifications like PMP, ITIL and CSP force your team to learn a broad set of best practices rather than focusing on a technology or technique they use every day.

How many members of your team have a good grip on statistics, economics, finance, project management, operating system design, or database design? In almost every community, colleges and universities welcome working professionals into individual classes or part-time programs compatible with a work schedule. I worked with a team that held a weekend programming competition to develop a high-performance text processing module just for fun. The results were not only tested but peer reviewed to share techniques and style.

But, why do you really care about this? First, you most likely have an IT department full of underperforming assets. IT is a competitive weapon and increasingly critical to basic business operations. To get the most out of your overall IT investment, you need your people performing at their best. IT knowledge work is part art and part science. It is very difficult to tell in advance what basic skill you might need, from network performance statistical analysis to a database failure root-cause analysis to selection of the best operating system to meet your strategic business objectives. If your bright young talent has become old and flabby, they will not be able to deliver to your expectations. I find many managers allow their team to underperform because they fill in all the gaps themselves. While this might be a strategy to keep personally fit, IT is a team effort and personal heroism is a bad strategy (chapter 13).

Raising the capability in any team member raises the total capability of the team and allows other team members to focus on their part of the effort. The largest risk in any IT project is human error. We are, after all, fallible beings. Exercising the basics prevents "I forgot" errors or errors that result from stretching too far. Although you can't eliminate all errors, the well-trained team falters less often. And if you're saddled with the wrong people (chapter 6), this is an opportunity to help them transform into the right ones.

I want to be very clear about what I mean by exercise. Keeping up with the latest technology is not the same as exercising the basics. I seem to meet the most out-of-touch technologists at trade shows and technology expos. Many IT professionals are gadget people. We like the coolest new gizmo and we develop bragging rights from knowing about the latest invention. There's nothing wrong with this knowledge in itself. It is akin to learning about a new sport or testing a demo tennis racquet or golf club. But, if you don't actually get out there and play, you aren't getting any exercise. Mental exercise should be as physically difficult as a good jog or long swim. A collection of facts does not constitute mental exercise, so don't count the portion of the training budget spent on fact-collection events as this kind of exercise.

> *I want to be very clear about what I mean by exercise. Keeping up with the latest technology is not the same as exercising the basics.*

Doctor's Orders

So what does the doctor prescribe? A healthy diet and a regular exercise program of course! First, get your IT team to consume good food. The industry produces hundreds of journals, books, articles, blogs, and other sources of information. Naturally, not all of these materials are a particularly good workout. You will have to be discerning and trial some periodicals and authors before judging them adequate for the task.

Fortunately, the Internet abounds with opinions on much of that material. Connect with local or online sources that can guide your team toward the best and most challenging material. Develop a library of strongly recommended reads and expect it to be used. But go beyond just a healthy diet; put that diet to work. If you ask your team to read a book, expect them to apply the material to a project and report what effect it had on the project. Encourage study and reward the application and sharing of what they have learned. Gather for team exercise like the coding competition and brown-bag study group I described earlier. But, most of all, get your IT team to learn about their business.

I am astounded by the number of IT people I encounter who lack any understanding of how their company functions. No matter the industry, get your IT people to ride along with marketing, operations, sales, manufacturing, etc. Set aside time for your team to spend a day or a week within a business area at least every quarter, and at as many levels as they can reasonably visit. Encourage your technically trained staff to earn an MBA to better balance their skills. Develop a "fly on the wall" seat for an IT staffer at senior

> *I am astounded by the number of IT people I encounter who lack any understanding of how their company functions. No matter the industry, get your IT people to ride along with marketing, operations, sales, manufacturing, etc.*

management meetings just to listen in and develop a feel for what is important to the business as a whole. Well-rounded training including business, technical, and leadership skills will produce results that will amaze you.

The Brown-Bag Book Club

I worked some years ago for a successful company that could manufacture and sell its popular products with a fairly small sales and administrative staff and thus a small IT department. Yes, we had data-center operations, a help desk, network support, and software development, but each of these teams was only a few members and the total IT department was fewer than thirty people.

Each had his assigned task, but in a small team you work in more than one area and often pitch in where help is needed. I was a software developer, but found myself in network wiring closets pulling cables, sitting in at the help desk, and helping the data center do root-cause analysis on production job issues. A small team that works well together makes for a great place to work and I enjoyed my job. In addition to good software development projects, I exercised my basic IT skills in many different areas, as did many of the team. Unfortunately, with such a small team, when it came to more structured exercise, we just didn't have the time individually or couldn't coordinate our calendars so we could get a group together for a game or other mental workout.

I've long been a proponent of keeping sharp in my industry, but I must admit that the solution to our workout problem didn't come from my passion for exercise. I had begun conducting facilitated design sessions on projects where we were inventing something. The business was in a program to significantly increase the profitability of the operation and we explored many new ideas for IT systems.

In a facilitated session, I needed a facilitator, a design consultant who knew the proposed technology to be used, a scribe, and members of the business community who owned the idea and drove the business requirements. As you might have guessed, we had neither the time nor the skills to fill all of these roles. I was the only trained facilitator in IT and we often encountered technologies with which we had very little experience or technologies on which I was the only in-house expert. I then couldn't facilitate with appropriate neutrality.

Fortunately, not only was the company's IT staff an intimate group, the town boasted only a few companies whose IT groups were officed locally. This meant that all of the IT people in town knew each other. We met at church, on the golf course, at our kids' sporting events, and at other venues. Most of us were at least acquainted. One of my friends was an IT manager at the local hospital. He suffered from the same problem of needing more skills than he had to really do a project right.

After some weeks of frustration about similar projects, we decided to try something new and trade resources across companies. None of the local firms were competitors. There was enough job hopping of the small pool of IT people that at least one person in each company had worked for at least one of the other companies town. There was little risk of sharing proprietary information, and we quickly settled this with a few confidentiality agreements. In short order, I was facilitating sessions for him and he was facilitating sessions for me. It didn't take long to get several other local firms involved and we developed a pool of talent that we exchanged with each other as needed.

As useful as this was as a way to get access to the right people, yet another unexpected positive effect emerged. As it turned out, several people in our pool of talent were part-time teachers at the local community college and very interested in maintaining their IT fitness. So, we started a lunchtime book club. We met in one of the larger corporate lunchrooms every week or so and studied and discussed a wide variety of texts. Sometimes we would have homework assignments, and once held a cross-company software development competition to draw more of our own teams into the workout.

These lunch sessions were a little like meeting at the gym for a game of basketball or some other team sport. We got a good mental workout. We were accountable to a group of friends who provided both positive and negative reinforcement to ensure we did our homework. We were connected to the latest thinking in several companies in widely different industries and also to the local community college where academic research and thinking was available through the fine state universities that supported the community college.

Because we were now exercising as a group, we knew the skills of the other members. If we struggled to improve or master a skill, someone else in the group could offer advice and coaching. It turned out to be an excellent way to exercise.

Get Out of Your Office

With this scale of operation, it became easy for IT staff members to focus on a particular specialty and to keep in shape only on the detailed skills needed for this narrow area of focus.

In my career journey, I had occasion to work in a multinational firm with extensive operations around the world, many different departments, and many different products manufactured, sold, and distributed. This firm's large IT department had a significant presence in four cities in the United States alone. With this scale of operation, it became easy for IT staff members to focus on a particular specialty and to keep in shape only on the detailed skills needed for this narrow area of focus. During the process of learning about the business, I was encouraged to visit various parts of the operation, which I did. I spent time in numerous departments and many locations. Within three years I had visited operations all over the world.

When I spoke about my experience with "the business," I quickly became a celebrity. Most of my peers had hardly left the IT offices during their career and few had ventured out of the state, not to mention out of the country. I found many IT associates who had such a small circle of contacts within the company that they had no idea how things really worked. They had grown into deeply skilled specialists. The biggest disappointment was that the company encouraged the exploration that would have exposed them to so many interesting facets of the operation.

Like any good training program, your IT fitness efforts must strengthen existing skills, as well as broaden your team's understanding of the technical and IT process areas as well as your business and industry. While working in the consumer packaged goods (CPG) industry, I regularly met with non-competing CPG companies and even went on route rides with their direct-store delivery drivers to better understand the industry as a whole. Encourage these kinds of activities, and ensure your IT staff takes the opportunity to do them.

Fitness Is Not Free

This brings us to the matter of budget. So far I have avoided talking about money by describing other ways you can handle some of the issues I've discussed, but here's where that stops. As an individual team member or a leader without budgetary control, you may have to make due with what you have, but for the rest of you budget for fitness. If you are going to maintain a reasonable level of productivity, if you want your team to operate at their best, if you plan to establish a consistent record of project success, you have to budget to sustain or grow your IT talent. This means having line items in the IT budget for developing career opportunities. This means purchasing a reference and workout library and budgeting the time for people to use it. This means giving your staff a rest after a particularly tough workout or a sustained effort.

Look into your IT budget and see if you have room for pre-season training, regular exercise during the game and enough down time to avoid injuries. Without these specified in your budget, your team will not do them and the money and time you thought you could use for this purpose will be spent on more "critical" items like sign-on bonuses for new members to replace the team you burned out before the project was complete.

I recently visited a CIO who was trying to fill an infrastructure manager position. Her operation was in an "international" location, meaning it was not in the same country as the corporate headquarters. She was having trouble filling this position because it was scheduled to be moved to a regional data center in two or three years. She did not have any talent on her team sufficient for the task because the team was expected to run very lean and she had no spare capacity to develop a broad base of talent.

In addition, because of the clear future of the position, internal team members who might have been candidates were moving to other roles to preserve their career path. Candidates in the local market were not interested in joining a company where they would have no future and she was faced with putting a contractor in a critical role.

The first thing that entered my mind was that the headquarters office had sufficient talent and someone would leap at the chance of working in a foreign country (fortunately one with the same native language), knowing that they could return to the home office after several years and be even further along in their career path. Unfortunately, neither the international location nor the home office had developed a specific budget for funding expatriates as a means of training and sustaining talent. Although the idea sounded interesting to all parties, money was tight, so the position remains unfilled. Make fitness a line item and fund it fully.

Chapter 10: Ignorance as a Defense

"I wish I didn't know now what I didn't know then."

— *Bob Seger*

In the post-Enron world, no longer can corporate executives claim ignorance as a defense. The Sarbanes-Oxley rules and increased scrutiny by investors are forcing senior executives to either really know what is going on or live with the consequences of their ignorance. Even if you do not work for a publicly held company, the standards for governance, transparency, and accountability continue to increase. Your IT investments not only require greater visibility and control, but also are themselves the means whereby you control your financial and operational systems.

We can no longer skimp on governance, compliance, and controls in IT systems. We have to constantly check to see what we might have missed. Even honest ignorance can send C-level executives to prison (if really bad things are going on). Ignorance at the corporate level has wide-reaching conse-quences, and generally results from ignorance at lower levels such as

> *Ignorance at the corporate level has wide-reaching consequences, and generally results from ignorance at lower levels such as at the individual IT project level.*

at the individual IT project level. If you use IT systems and don't really know what they are controlling and how they interact, if you are responsible for IT investments and you don't really know if project controls are protecting your company's assets, if you are an

IT project manager or team member and you don't really know if the developers are creating back doors to circumvent controls (even with good intent), then you have a form of ignorance that could well topple the company if someone with bad intent does know these things.

I find ignorance of two kinds in the organizations I encounter. The first is ignorance of controls best-practices and what is really going on inside IT projects. For most publicly traded companies, SOX compliance has forced the IT department to develop both awareness and skills in this area. But, for many smaller projects or organizations not directly affected by SOX, IT controls are often ignored.

The second kind of ignorance I encounter is what I call second-order ignorance, or 2OI. If first-order ignorance is not knowing (and knowing that you don't know), second-order ignorance is not knowing what you don't know. If this concept is a little hard to grasp, don't worry, I will explain it in more detail later in this chapter. Both kinds of ignorance are a threat to the success of your IT projects, but fortunately both can be managed.

Maintaining Control

Due to government and investor pressure, compliance, controls, and governance best-practice is going to improve to some degree over time, at least in the U.S. and nations that follow similar investment governance. As we learn to cope with regulatory changes, we will more effectively integrate transparency, separation of duties, traceability, and other controls into systems development in large public companies. Those practices will become the standard, and poor governance will become the exception rather than the rule. For large companies and large IT investments, this is already happening and is even being used as a point of competitive advantage. However, it will be some time before the expertise being developed on extremely visible projects trickles down to all IT projects and then moves into companies that are not publicly held.

You may be satisfied to wait, thinking that you will not be affected by any of this for a long time. Consider this: Senior executives do tend to move around a bit. Those who are growing accustomed to a disciplined IT operation will share their experiences with others and will demand more discipline as they move to organizations not yet affected by regulatory change. The need to eliminate executive ignorance will move far faster than IT practices. It is cheaper to build in solid controls now than it will be to retrofit them in the near future.

Executives, particularly in the area of finance, are finding that the discipline of well-managed change control, project audits, and functional governance plans are reducing risk in IT projects and helping to identify bad investments early so good money is not invested on top of bad money. They are going to demand the same level of comfort when they move to other companies, whether those companies require SOX compliance or not. In addition, as lending institutions, investors, donors, and customers find greater comfort in companies that have proven themselves to be well con-trolled, they will ensure their money goes to those companies. If you are still blissfully ignorant of this area of IT, it is time to wake up before a lack of discipline results in a corporate disaster.

Whether you work in a highly disciplined environment or your IT shop is a group of coding cowboys, the steps to better control are the same:

1. Determine where you are.

2. Pick something to work on.

3. Communicate the new standard.

4. Review work that needs to meet the new standard.

These steps can be very simple if you are just getting started, and much more formal and detailed if you are a mature IT shop (from a governance perspective).

1. Determine where you are

To determine where you are, start with an audit. If your shop doesn't conduct regular audits, you have two choices. You can ask for your corporate audit group or an outside auditor to conduct an audit, or you can simply make a quick assessment yourself. As you have seen, Russ and I are big fans of keeping things simple. If you have never done an IT audit — particularly around governance and controls — you may not be ready for the shock of finding out where you are on the scale of out-of-control to well-managed. Additionally, the level of detail you will get from an audit, not to mention the price tag, can be overwhelming.

Simply sitting your team around a table and looking for the most common risks that occur across all projects will help you identify candidates for project governance. A two-hour conversation between your group and a specialist on corporate controls such as separation of duties or traceability will help you brainstorm some current practices you should modify.

One of my clients was a large utility company. It was just coming to grips with the age of energy deregulation and its security group was asked to conduct informal audits of various aspects of their organization to identify high-risk practices they could change quickly and easily before doing a full audit of the business. I specialized in a particular platform on which they ran their email system, internal websites and some business-to-business applications available through the Internet. Because of this experience, they asked if I would be willing to do a quick security assessment of their IT systems and practices around this platform. My specialty is systems architecture and design. I know a little about many things in the IT arena, but am not so foolish to consider myself an expert on all topics, so I brought in a friend whose business focused on the security aspects of this particular platform.

We spent two days taking a look at their organization, processes, tools, and the state of their systems. We also developed a map that compared where they thought they were to where we thought they were to help them understand that perception is not reality (chapter 12). I won't go into the detailed findings, but I can say that they were extremely happy that this was not a formal audit or several of them may have found themselves looking for new opportunities elsewhere. One finding that was particularly troublesome (but not uncommon) was that we were able to easily find the system IDs and guess or crack all the administrator-level passwords (with one exception). Even if you are not a IT security professional, you can guess the kind of damage we could have caused if we had used one of those IDs.

2. Pick something to work on

There's more to the story, but it has led us to the second step: Pick something to work on. However you do your assessment to determine where you are, you need to compare the findings against risks. I suggest you consider ongoing process improvement as a project in itself, but at a minimum create a separate risk matrix (chapter 8) to help prioritize your findings. You only need to concern yourself with the top risks. I tend to use the top ten, but you can decide how many to evaluate.

After you have them in order, spend some time exploring what it will take to avoid each risk altogether. Then balance the risk score (impact times likelihood) with the effort to correct it and select the top one, two, or three to tackle. Unless you already have a well-disciplined organization, do not attempt to tackle more than three at a time. You can pick up the others after you have had some success with the most important ones. One of the cardinal rules of problem solving is that as soon as you solve problem number-one, problem number-two gets a promotion. There will always be a top problem to solve and, at least at the outset, solving number-one can make a pretty big difference.

We helped facilitate the process for the client and they developed an understanding of the kind of work that would be necessary to correct their top issues. The team set out on a six-month project to correct the most egregious security risks. As I recommended earlier, they worked on only a few problems at a time, and expected to be able to move through the list in about six months. We set a date for a follow-up visit and mini-audit to see how they were progressing on those issues.

3. Communicate the new standard

My client also executed Step 3. They published the overall results and developed some simple and clear guidelines describing the new standards. These standards were shared at team meetings, sent in newsletters, and added to the official standards documents.

4. Review the work to meet the new standard

Exactly how you communicate changes in standards is your decision. However, Step 3 is nothing without Step 4, and I recommend that when you communicate a new standard, you also communicate how work will be reviewed for compliance. If you publish the standard alone, you are unlikely to get people to change their behavior. To drive that change, tell them how their work will be checked. My client did a great job with Steps 1-3, but failed miserably on Step 4.

The problem of the administrator IDs and passwords was at the top of their list of things to fix. The security and system administrator teams were going to make it much more difficult to get a list of system IDs. Because the administrator IDs had been public for so long, they were going to change the IDs for every administrator. To better protect their passwords, they were going to change the encryption system so stored passwords could not be decrypted or easily broken with dictionary attacks. Each administrator would change his password using a set of strong password guidelines. We shared these new practices with the administration team, as well as with the computer users of the company at large. To encourage ID and password change, our published findings even included a list of the old administrator IDs and passwords.

When we arrived for our follow-up visit, we started at the top of the list. We looked for system IDs and found them much more difficult to see. This was good news and set high expectations. Since we could no longer see the IDs, we assumed they had changed. To check, we opened our report from the first visit and attempted to login using the old IDs and passwords. By using a list of the twenty most common passwords found in our previous work, we were able to confirm that none of the administrators had changed their ID. We were also able to guess the passwords of all but one of them — the same one as before — in about fifteen minutes. Despite being published, some of the passwords had not changed since our first visit.

At that point we stopped our audit. If they had not solved problem number one, there was no point in wasting their money checking the rest of the list. We reserved a conference room and called a meeting of all the administrators and the leaders who were responsible for implementing the proposed changes. We set up a butcher block tablet on a tripod so it was impossible not to notice as people entered the room. On the front sheet we wrote the passwords of all of the administrators with no other text indicating what the list might be. As you might expect, it was obvious to all what the list was and each administrator could see that their password was on the list. Nobody had done a good job with this change in security controls. It was a shamed and guilt-ridden group that gathered around the conference table. When all were present, we simply said that they all knew the results of the audit and when they were serious about doing the work we would be happy to come back and check their work again.

They never called us back. One of the reasons for this was the strong organizational support for hero syndrome. During our initial visit, it became clear that members of the team who could become noticed for doing "extra" work, were rewarded. No attention was given to those who did their work well and went home on time. Only those who were seen working a weekend, or who developed a flashy piece of software (no matter that it exposed the organization to huge security risks) were noticed. The one administrator whose password we could not crack also had secured the servers and applications in her area and had followed security best-practices throughout her span of control. The associates she supported worked in a more stable environment, reporting fewer issues to the help desk. However, she was not a hero and had fallen from notice.

Her peers, however, were constantly competing to be noticed. When we posted their passwords — effectively calling them incompetent — we took the wind from their capes. A continued relationship with us would further expose their poor practices and serve to dispel the hero aura that surrounded them. Since the organization was not going to reward good security practices, these heroes did not want to be in a position where they would be punished for the way they currently operated, but seeing no reward for the effort needed to change. The easiest solution was to remove the people who were exposing the problem.

The problems you tackle will be specific to your organization, its risks, and your need for compliance and governance. Thus, it is impossible for us to give specific advice on how to measure and how to check every change you might make. Nonetheless, one of the tools we use covers a wide variety of issues. My utility company client would have had much more success with Step 4, and the project as a whole, had they employed this simple tool. It is the peer review.

Tool: Peer Review

In the IT world, a peer review is synonymous with a code review, meaning the peer review of a software program in its original computer language. While I mean exactly that for code, I use the term peer review because you should review everything you possibly can — not just code — using a peer review.

For a detailed guide on reviews get a copy of the *Handbook of Walkthroughs, Inspections, and Technical Reviews*[10]. In brief, a peer review is a short meeting to review all or a part of any deliverable that can be rendered in printed form. A developer, project manager, or other author of the deliverable submits their final version to whomever is managing the review process and a peer team is selected. Peers are those whose current work or previous experience makes them capable of understanding the form of the work product to be reviewed (e.g., computer language, diagram or model, design document, etc.) and whose role on the project or in the organization makes them able to review the content as it applies to the business problem (chapter 5).

A peer review team is convened for a single review, although you might have a regular group of peer reviewers if you expect a significant volume of similar material. The review team should be no less than three and no more than seven individuals. The review team does not include the author of the document. The author should not be present at the review meeting, if that is at all possible — the work product should speak for itself. If the author is there aiding understanding and providing clarification, it is impossible to tell if the document could do its job without the author to help it along.

Each of the reviewers should receive the document in advance and be required to read and evaluate it before the meeting. They

---

[10] Freedman, Daniel P. and Gerald M. Weinberg. *Handbook of Walkthroughs, Inspections and Technical Reviews: Evaluation Programs, Projects, and Products.* Third Edition. New York: Dorset House, 1990.

are not to share their comments until the meeting, but doing the pre-work is essential for an effective peer review. The meeting itself should be 15-30 minutes. Designate one of the reviewers to facilitate the group. The group should discuss the correctness, adherence to standards, and quality attributes of the work they are evaluating. The facilitator must keep the meeting tightly focused and the work product must be small enough (break it up into several reviews if necessary) that no review process is longer than 30 minutes.

The outcome of the meeting is twofold. First, the work product is: accepted, accepted with minor changes, or rejected. If it is rejected, it is returned to the author with comments from the reviewers detailing why it failed the review. If it is accepted with minor changes, the changes are noted and the author is expected to make the changes, but is not required to resubmit the work product for review. In addition, if the work is accepted or accepted with changes, the peer review team assumes responsibility for correctness, adherence to standards, and quality. Should the work product fail to produce as expected, the author is no longer responsible. That responsibility has been transferred to the peer review team.

Holding the peer review team responsible

It takes some effort to really make the responsibility part of the review process work, but without it your reviews are a farce. It is vital that the review team have a stake in their decision. If you do not have sufficient peers, as in the story I am about to tell, hire some from the outside or recruit some from other parts of your organization. Get an agreement in advance that, if they approve something and it fails, they are responsible for correcting the failure on their own time and at their own expense.

Many years ago, I worked on a project that entailed building an electronic document portfolio of materials related to U.S. Food and Drug Administration (FDA) regulated clinical trials for pharmaceuticals. As part of this project, I was tasked with making an electronic signature mechanism compliant with the FDA electronic signature guidelines. This was no small task and, in the end, it involved a relatively small, but technically deep piece of software that would extend the internal workings of their electronic document platform to guarantee both security protection and traceability.

I spent several weeks researching and developing the design of this component and made a presentation to the team. None of the team had the deep systems knowledge or the programming skills to understand the details of the solution, but everyone could grasp the overall design and approach to closing the gap that we had in the underlying platform. I presented the solution at a high level of abstraction in order to communicate what I was going to do. However, this was not a peer review because I had no real technical peers on the team. Don't misinterpret this statement as arrogance about my technical prowess. I have no doubt many others could have done an equal or better job designing this component; however, the point is that none of those people were on our team or participated in the design review.

I then went on to build the component. I was a consultant and was not given the budget to do pair-programming or use techniques that would put more than one person on the task, so I did it all myself. Because the work was challenging for me, I called in a few favors and asked for others to check my work as I went along. However, these informal checks did not constitute a formal review and, for the most part, the client did not know I was getting a second opinion on any of the work. We went through the formal testing and production implementation steps but, because nobody really understood the technical details, I wrote the test scripts and implementation plan. It was pretty much a one-man show.

The test scripts were based on the overall requirements and, as far as anyone could tell, the gap we needed to close was closed and the system did what it was supposed to do. What nobody could say for sure — they took my word for it — was whether the system did anything it was not supposed to do. Because of how I connected the component into the kernel of the document-management platform, I could have written many back doors into the system without anyone's knowledge. By adding this control, I could have created a mechanism to circumvent other controls without corrupting the electronic signatures, thereby invalidating the entire system. The customer trusted me and had a release deadline to meet, so my pleas to have a true peer review fell on deaf ears.

Knowing what you know now, would you take that risk? Ignorance, in this case, could mean errors in clinical trials, opening the door to lawsuits, fraud, and even death. In an otherwise highly structured organization (or at least the part that conducted clinical trials), the IT group was running amok with corporate-level risk in a very competitive industry where consumers lives were on the line.

If you have a well-exercised team, are solving the right problem, measuring the right things, and managing risk, you will find that one risk always appears on your chart: the black hole of the unknown.

Second-Order Ignorance

The more difficult ignorance problem to tackle is second-order ignorance. If you have a well-exercised team (chapter 9), are solving the right problem (chapter 5), measuring the right things (chapter 7), and managing risk (chapter 8), you will find that one risk always appears on your chart: the black hole of the unknown. For years, I put "gotcha" or something similar on my risk matrix, because it always seemed that something completely unexpected would reach out and slap my project around. I worked with a technology manager who told me the rule of estimates was to add three (of whatever is the base measure) and double it. If someone told him a project would take two weeks, he would add three weeks and double it for a total of ten. If he was told $40,000 he would add $30,000 and double it for a total of $140,000. He rarely missed deadlines or exceeded his budget, but what he was really doing was coping with second-order ignorance. The problem is you don't know what you don't know, so how do you manage this risk?

I was the Chief Technology Officer of a technology start-up. We had our first product installed at several locations and were working on two more products. Naturally we were continuing to enhance product number-one and the three products would form the core of our offering. The firm was anxious to hit the corner of the "hockey stick" — that place on the revenue graph where successful start-ups begin moving from very small growth to really huge growth. But, before we could get there, we needed all three products complete.

The CEO was a salesman and particularly anxious to be able to see progress. The sales, marketing, and operations staff was housed on one side of the floor we rented, with the R&D, development, and support staff on the other. A stairwell separated the two sides, giving him one path to get to the development team. My office door was at the end of the short hallway separating the offices and the development group worked further inside. At least daily, the CEO would stride down the hallway, walk directly past my office, and lean over a developer's shoulder to see what was going on with the product that day. Even in a small company, when the CEO stands behind you, all work ceases. The developer would answer the CEO's questions and show him several features (which had hardly changed since yesterday). After he had satiated his curiosity, the CEO would then come to my office to discuss what was really going on. In this way, I was losing hours of precious development time each week.

I needed to find a way to satisfy his need to know without disturbing the staff. Obviously my regular status reports to the executives and the board were not doing the trick. There is, I must admit, something very satisfying about seeing things first-hand. Nonetheless, I had to stop the incessant interruptions.

Russ and I had developed a set of tools around a framework (which we'll describe in chapter 14) and we were wrestling with the issue of risk management for 2OI. My start-up company seemed the perfect place to test the concept. I posted three 2OI charts, Figure 6, in the hallway and gave each cell a color indicating a status of complete, in-progress, and yet to begin. Executives are suckers for pretty charts and my CEO was no exception. The next day, as he came down the hall to interrupt my developers, he came to an abrupt halt in front of the charts. Each was labeled with the product name and each had a different total in large numbers. He could see that they meant something important because the product most near completion had the smallest number. My office was his next stop. This time, there were no developer interruptions. Hurray!

	What	How	Where	Who	When	Why
Scope (Idea)	25	25	25	25	25	25
Context (Proposal)	20	20	20	20	20	20
Logical (Req./PMP)	15	15	15	15	15	15
Physical (Design)	10	10	10	10	10	10
Construct (Develop)	5	5	5	5	5	5
Total						**450**

Figure 6: 2OI matrix template

I spent five minutes explaining how we used the chart, in much the same way I will explain to you in the following paragraphs. We went back to the charts to talk about specific areas of second-order ignorance where his sales and operations teams could help us close some of gaps that remained. After our talk he went back to his side of the building. I kept the charts updated and, for the most part, he stopped visiting the developers. Not only was the tool helping us manage risk, but it had worked perfectly as a means to communicate an important aspect of the project. It also gave us a focus for directing the work of others who were motivated to speed our progress.

Tool: Second-Order-Ignorance Matrix

Here's how Russ and I set up the charts. One of the concepts that makes handling something as difficult to grasp as 2OI is that not everything matters in the context of a project. The realm of the unknown that we care about is finite. There are some things we don't know that won't affect our project. If we can put a fence around all the 2OI we care about, perhaps we could manage the risk. After much time and trial at building fences, we found that one was already built. It is the Zachman Framework[11]. While John Zachman had enterprise architecture in mind, we have found his framework to be excellent for managing 2OI. Our version of the framework looks like figure 6.

The concept is that each cell contains things you don't know that you don't know. By selecting the cells that matter to your project, and doing a little digging — we have developed tools for this (chapter 14), but just knowing you have to look for 2OI is often enough — your job is to discover what you don't know and then manage that first-order ignorance as you would any other risk. The columns are obviously the six interrogatives you must answer to develop a complete understanding of any thing or event: who, what, when, where, why, and how. The order of the interrogatives corresponds to John Zachman's framework.

The rows represent a perspective and roughly correspond to the most common phases in an IT project. Just answering the question "who" is not enough. You have to explore who from each perspective

---

[11] Zachman, John and Samuel Holcman. *Zachman Framework for Enterprise Architecture*. The Zachman Institute for Framework Advancement. <www.zifa.com>

to be sure you have eliminated second-order ignorance completely. We use some of the tools described in the first 13 chapters to help us understand the perspective and interrogative in a particular cell. You can see where they fit in the overall framework in chapter 14.

The numbers in the matrix correspond to an overall 2OI risk factor. Since second-order ignorance for a database schema (the physical implementation of a database) is less risky than second-order ignorance at the strategy level (should I have a database at all?) the numbers are larger at the top of the chart and smaller at the bottom. As you become confident that you have done sufficient work within a cell to eliminate 2OI — or at least enough to eliminate the risk of finding more — remove the number from the cell. Each eliminated 2OI cell reduces the total at the bottom of the grid.

Your second-order ignorance shrinks correspondingly. In my highly non-scientific experience, when a project's 2OI score falls below about 100, the likelihood and impact of 2OI as a risk is reduced sufficiently to fall off your risk matrix. We've found that, at the 100 point, the remaining 2OI will be found through the natural progression of your project and the looming, high-impact "gotchas" have been eliminated.

Reading this section has now caused a problem for you. Previously, you might not have known that you didn't know how to manage second-order ignorance. Now you do.

In my first use of the tool at the start-up company, the goal was mostly to reduce the number of CEO visits to the R&D and development areas. However, I found that the increased awareness of 2OI, and the clear way the matrix communicates 2OI, significantly adds value to the tool. We were unsure what the total really meant until we had further experience with the tool. Along the way, we discovered that the 100 mark seemed to feel right, not only at my start-up company but in other places where we have used the matrix since then.

Reading this section has now caused a problem for you. Previously, you might not have known that you didn't know how to manage 2OI. Now you do. You now have first-order ignorance about your project's second-order ignorance. My advice: Do what is necessary to improve your governance and compliance practices, trap 2OI and stay alert. Ignorance is not a defense.

Chapter 11: Ostrichism (Ignoring Complexity)

"I've made up my mind. Don't confuse me with the facts."

— *U.S. Representative Earl F. Landgreeb*

Sometimes ignorance is not the problem. You know the ugly truth but refuse to confront it. Ostrichism[12], or putting your head in the sand, is the term we give to those who will not confront the ugly truths facing their IT project. If you are solving the wrong problem (chapter 5) or measuring the wrong things (chapter 7) you don't really have the ugly truth so you are operating in ignorance (chapter 10) and need to fix that problem first. For those of you who are ostriches — and you know who you are — it is time to face facts and shed the fear that immobilizes you. When the truth is ugly and scary and difficult to take — that's when you need to confront it and neither ignore it nor brush it off as inconsequential.

The first step to facing the facts is getting the facts. You must develop a mechanism for ensuring that you are getting the truth, the whole truth and nothing but the truth. I have seen several otherwise competent project managers fail because they never knew how bad things really were. Had they known, they would have applied themselves to

[12] Kahn, Herman. *Thinking About the Unthinkable*. New York: Avon Books, 1962.

dealing with the situation. Sometimes you are an unwitting ostrich simply because you only see glowing reports of project success and never dig deeper to see if the "glow" is legitimate. If this is a problem in your organization, find a way to get the data you need.

I once attended a project review meeting where the project manager had designated one team member as the "purveyor of doom." This person's job was to tell everyone how bad it really was before all of the glowing reports rolled in. Because there was some humor in the role, the messenger wasn't blamed for

> *I once attended a project review meeting where the project manager had designated one team member as the "purveyor of doom." This person's job was to tell everyone how bad it really was before all of the glowing reports rolled in.*

the message and the group was able to then tone-down overstated successes and focus on problem areas. Whatever your method, get to the truth.

Once you have the bad news, revisit your risk matrix (chapter 8) and manage the effects of the ugly truth. It is critical that you do not keep this information to yourself. If the overall project risk profile has changed drastically or if you are in a hole with no way out, get this information to those with the power to either kill the project before greater losses are incurred or change the parameters so you have some chance of success. If you suspect that your concerns will be ignored, be prepared to discuss the specific impact the problem will have on your project. A decision maker will listen to, "The failure of this technology will cause a six-week delay and cost us $100,000" much more seriously than, "If the xyz dongle throws a 601x error, the entire project will implode!!"

Financial Factors

Faulty financial thinking sometimes leads to ostrichism. The faulty financial logic is that after significant investment in a project some attempt to salvage the investment should be made, even when that attempt appears hopeless. Whole courses in strategic finance are taught around this problem, but I'll try to keep it to the essence: Don't throw good money after bad.

IT projects are structured generally as a series of unrecoverable costs. As soon as you do some portion of work, that cost is sunk whether or not the project ever produces. With some clever contracts and cost-juggling you can hedge or transfer risk, but on most projects such effort is far less profitable than regular appraisals of your IT investment portfolio (ongoing projects). Front-loading your risks (chapter 8) and evaluating the project honestly on a regular basis actually lets you minimize valueless investments by avoiding throwing money away on lost causes.

I observed a large corporation for several years. They had a history of taking IT projects to completion even if those projects were clearly not going to produce a return. This included several very painful examples of throwing good money after bad and reinvesting in an attempt to turn already failed projects around. Some new leadership recognized this issue and set up a project management office to bring better practices to managing the extensive IT portfolio. Although my role in this organization was not to introduce "process," I can't watch from the sidelines as others work to correct these habits without occasionally lending a tidbit of advice.

After a considerable length of time — large organizations do not change deeply imbedded habits quickly — I was in a senior management project review where several projects were being evaluated. My project was one of these and I was selected to represent the project team, thick skin being the primary selection criteria for the task. Fortunately, our work was generally on track and I didn't expect much interaction when it was my turn so I was able to enjoy the rest of the review. One project in particular was slated to spend several million dollars in total and had already consumed $450,000 in expenses. The project was at a critical decision point and the project lead had the courage to recommend the project be scrapped. From the work they had already done, it appeared that the anticipated benefits could not be delivered and the team saw no way forward. The choice facing the executive review board was whether to press on as planned (the old habit), or kill the project after a $450,000 sunk cost. After some probing to determine if the team had really done adequate due diligence on their recommendation, the executive committee canceled the project and further investment, and set up a meeting to discuss dispersing the team to other projects.

I was impressed. No blame was laid on the project team. Nobody was fired or demoted or stuck on a bad project for punishment. The executive team calmly accepted the results of the work done thus far, considered the expense a sunk cost, and prevented the organization from incurring greater losses. The meeting proceeded to the next project up for review as smoothly as if the canceled project had been reported as a stunning success. This is the way IT projects are supposed to fail — early and with dignity.

In organizations not ready to accept failure as a natural part of high-risk investment (which is what IT projects are), truthfulness in communication may break down. The worst side-effect of ostrichism inside a project is the likelihood that the next layer up in organizational management is full of unwitting ostriches that "don't want to hear bad news." Poor reaction to bad news, minimizing the downsides, or being too attentive to those providing a positive spin to everything will inhibit the movement of important information. If your business is so dysfunctional that you are fired for presenting rational facts to the decision makers, then you should welcome the forced change of venue.

You also need to be careful not make a molehill out of a mountain. Sometimes complex problems are just that: complex. Too often, I have reviewed project analyses and reports that minimize problems in the hopes that I would consider them unimportant and the project team could carry on without really dealing with the complexity of the problem. Good risk management should prevent this but, if your assessment of a risk was naïve or fell short of the real impact of the issue, don't cover that up. Again, get that information to people who can help develop a complex (or sometimes even simple) solution to your complex problem.

The real solution to ostrichism is to face the music. Bad news hurts, but getting the right people working the problem early and doing good risk management can often help you recover from what may seem an impossible situation. Also get the decision makers involved, perhaps more resources or a change in the timeline for promised value can be negotiated if the risk profile of the overall project is not too badly damaged. As Russ likes to remind me: Face the music and you may find that it really is danceable.

Classic Anti-Ostrichism

I read about this story in Jim Collins' book *Good to Great*[13] and decided to research it myself. I found it a fascinating view into one of the reasons Winston Churchill was so effective as a war leader. During World War II, Winston Churchill was very serious about getting the facts and making sure that, regardless of the message, he got the honest truth as best as could be determined with the available information[14]. When he took over the Admiralty in 1939, he established a Statistical Department[15] — sometimes referred to as the Statistical branch. He staffed it with a colleague, Professor Lindemann and about a half-dozen like-minded statisticians and economists. Churchill makes it clear that he and Lindemenn agreed on the need for brutally honest information before starting the department and Lindemann appeared to operate to Churchill's satisfaction throughout the war. Churchill carried the same group of people with him as Prime Minister and used their materials extensively, often referring to their material in memoranda and directives[16].

[13] Collins, Jim. *Good to Great*. New York: HarperCollins, 2001.

[14] Churchill, Winston. *The Second World War, Volume 1: The Gathering Storm*. London: Cassell & Co., 1948. Page 421.

[15] Churchill, Winston. *The Churchill War Papers, vol. 2*. Gilbert, Martin, ed. New York: W. W. Norton & Company, 1995. Page xvii.

[16] Churchill, Winston. *The Churchill War Papers vol. 2*. Gilbert, Martin, ed. New York: W. W. Norton & Company, 1995. Page 1065.

The department was established to ensure that Churchill came face-to-face with the facts. The department was beholden to no one else in the government, so there was no one to encourage it to put a "good face" on the data for the sake of another department or individual. Churchill's interest was an honest assessment of the facts. To prevent the department from pandering to what it thought he wanted to hear, Churchill asked it to check and recheck facts frequently. He ensured they had access to all available material necessary to make a complete analysis and established their work as the standard for delivery to the Allies. In a memo to various departments, he encouraged them to come to a consensus on war figures, but relied on his own Statistical Department as the final word on any war-related data.

Churchill's Statistical Department did more than produce reports with numbers. They developed visual aids for understanding the data. Churchill had learned from the mistakes of World War I and did not want to repeat failures to properly supply the front lines due to a lack of good information. Lindemenn often developed materials to Churchill's specifications, but the department clearly understood not only how to analyze the data but how to present it in a meaningful form.

If your organization is highly compartmentalized or tends toward data that is skewed, you need to establish your own Statistical Department and get the facts yourself. Even if you are fairly certain that you have a grip on IT project reality, periodically check your sources and ensure nothing is being filtered out that should remain as part of the project status.

The Problem of Complexity

I have worked in a number of organizations where ostrichism is not an instinctive reaction to danger, but a result of complexity. In these organizations nobody intentionally sticks their head in the sand, but the complexity of the organization means that people are constantly working in a sandstorm. Being blinded by complexity is every bit as crippling as intentional ignorance.

I once assisted a corporate-level project office that reviewed IT project proposals. It was their job to determine if an investment was redundant with another project, if it had been done before, if there was an existing "better way," and if the proposed approach could be used to solve a problem in another business group. The main problem was that each business unit was fiercely autonomous. Long-entrenched general managers ran businesses in their own way, using local IT systems, local business processes, and local people under local control. The only projects that crossed corporate desks were those above a capital expenditure threshold, and the local IT teams had become quite skilled at preventing projects from reaching that threshold.

When the corporate office did see a proposal, it was shrouded in mystery. Interfaces to systems contained acronyms only understood by the local team. Business processes were given locally unique codenames. Common vocabulary meant different things in different groups. The local IT teams were not antagonistic toward the project office reviewing their proposals. But, at the same time, they had no incentive to reveal anything about their local operation. If corporate found that some systems developed under separate proposals would have been above the capital threshold when combined, this could cause trouble in the closely controlled local fiefdom. The corporate group had no budget for deep fact-finding and no political power to influence the local groups. Entering the corporate project office was like walking into a fog. They were completely incapable of doing their job because they couldn't see anything.

Our first action together was to assess what they could actually do with the resources and information they had. We determined that the group probably had about a one-year grace period when they could have little to no effect on the IT investment process and nobody would really notice. As long as there was apparent activity, they had time to get their act together. Using that cushion of time, we developed a plan to manage the complexity.

Of the locally autonomous groups, only ten were likely to propose projects relevant to the corporate team. The corporate team had six members who spent most of their time trying to figure out what was going on in the local groups. We decided to take a year off from accomplishing anything and concentrate on gathering information. Each of the team members would spend one or two six-month periods as part of a local team. We worked with the local IT managers to find an assignment where they would be completely under local control four days per week and would work on their corporate assignment one day per week. This meant that the local group got an additional, nearly full-time person at no cost. It was fairly easy to arrange. A few of the groups were in other cities so we had to get approval for several members to travel, but we agreed to take it out of existing expense and training budgets.

Because the goal was information-gathering, the local assignment was irrelevant to our scheme as long as our team member could handle the work. The team member's corporate assignment was to develop three deliverables to bring back when their tour was complete: a dictionary of local terminology and acronyms from both a business and IT perspective; an inventory of systems and the business problems they solved; and a diagram of the relationships among people such that we could see not only formal structures but track the movement of information and understand political influence. Because most of the information-gathering actually occurred while performing their local duties, Friday — the one day a week devoted to their corporate assignment — was spent documenting and conferring across the team to share what they had learned and plan for next weeks action.

The plan was a success. The following year, the team was able to improve enough IT investments to justify their year of relative inaction, and the team became a hub of influence. Through its time in the local businesses, it had become one of the few places at the corporate level where facts about the local groups were known or could be ascertained. Over the years, several of the original team members moved into prominent positions and credit this growth to their time building local relationships and understanding the wider business.

You may not be able to duplicate this particular method in your organization, but if you are faced with a sandstorm of complexity blocking you from needed facts, you may be able to find a way around or even through the problem. As this organization found, it was worth the effort to combat unintended ostrichism both from an IT project perspective and from the value gained by the individuals on the team.

Chapter 12: Giving Perception Sway (Not Communicating Reality)

The previous chapter dealt with the accuracy and usability of information coming in, and how that information is communicated up the chain of command. This chapter deals with the same problem, but in the opposite direction: how that information about the project is disseminated to subordinates, peers, and curious bystanders. As the brutal truth must flow upward, reality must flow outward. This does not mean that you must at all times share the brutal truth. Sometimes you hold onto some of the information to preserve a necessary advantage or prevent speculation. However, at no time should you encourage misperception.

I have often heard it said that, "Perception is reality." I'm sorry, but I disagree. Perception is perception and reality is reality. If you want someone's concept of reality — their perception — to be consistent with reality, you have to communicate reality. Too often we are trapped by the perceptions we create when we soften the blow of bad news on the project or provide too much fanfare for the good news. When one or more groups have inconsistent perceptions of your project, you are not getting the truth out in a clear and consistent manner.

As we have shown several times already, hero syndrome that is rewarded is often behavior that is misunderstood. When a project hero is needed, it is usually as a result of an error or poor planning, thus project heroism should be considered a sign of fundamental problems in the project. Your IT team is observed working weekends and the message communicated is that you have a dedicated team. Perhaps you have an incompetent team, or maybe you are asking for the impossible. Sometimes a surge of effort is the result of good planning and your IT team is mitigating a risk. Without clear communication, you may have trouble knowing the difference between heroism worthy of praise and heroism covering for errors or bad planning.

> *When a project hero is needed, it is usually as a result of an error or poor planning, thus project heroism should be considered a sign of fundamental problems in the project.*

Communicating Reality

If you don't clearly communicate reality, people involved or interested in your project will create a perception based on their own observations and decide it is reality. We're used to this in product positioning and perception building in marketing. If you create a new beverage and use enough advertising to position it as cool, people will believe it. However, if the product is actually bitter and nauseating, eventually the market will find out and no amount of advertising will help. With IT projects, it is so much easier to "position" because much of your audience neither understands nor has visibility into the details. Often you can maintain your "position" until very late in the project when you face more visible milestones. I have been in many organizations were this is the usual and customary pattern of behavior.

On the other hand, your project might be going well, but just as a poor product can be positioned in a better light so can a good product be positioned as a failure by the competition. Whether by design or by accident, I have witnessed several projects fail as a result of false perceptions held by decision makers. The problem is that if you don't tell them what you are doing, they will decide for themselves and they will be wrong. One of the most common failures on otherwise well-run projects is a lack of clear and unambiguous communication. Some of this ambiguity is a result of ignorance (chapter 10) or ostrichism (chapter 11); however, most is simply poor communications discipline. To develop good communications discipline, follow these guidelines:

- Let the data speak for itself.
- Understand that what you said might not be what they heard.
- Go easy; sometimes the truth hurts.

1. Let the data speak for itself

Two witnesses will often report a crime quite differently because their perspective and perception of the events usually differs. However, the DNA evidence doesn't have a bias. It is what it is. This is not to say that the interpretation of the data never varies, but the data itself cannot be denied. If you are trying to support an assertion without the support of data, I question your motives. If you have the data, I can question your interpretation, but I ignore the data at my peril. Let the data speak for itself as much as possible.

You may find yourself with a lack of data once in a while. But for all of those other times, don't attempt to communicate reality by eloquence alone. Use the data and let others make their own conclusions. Of course, you have to measure the right things (chapter 7) for your data to be valuable, but assuming you are, use that data.

2. Understand that what you said might not be what they heard

Next, remember that what you said might not be what they heard. In addition to a proclivity to misunderstand that is part of the human condition, we exacerbate the problem by adding ambiguity in lingo and technique. Because I am in the IT field, I felt for many years that we in IT are particularly fond of special vocabulary, acronyms, and phraseology that were intended to cause confusion and set us apart as a special breed. However, I have discovered that we are not unique in this regard. Almost all parts of the business carry a large arsenal of special vocabulary. If you remember the story from chapter 5 what the insiders considered very basic information and clear speaking was unintelligible to an educated young lady.

We in IT are particularly fond of special vocabulary, acronyms, and phraseology that were intended to cause confusion and set us apart as a special breed.

In chapter 5, we introduced the project dictionary as a tool to aid with clear communication. Unfortunately, having a dictionary does not mean your audience has read it or agrees with your definitions. Where you must use IT or business lingo, intersperse the definitions for those who aren't reading your dictionary. Better still, communicate the facts in common and unambiguous terms. You may be surprised to find how much easier it is to communicate when you avoid your convenient, but specialized, business vocabulary.

As I write this in the evenings, I am engaged during the day with an SAP® project. For those of you who have lived through an Enterprise Resource Planning (ERP) project using SAP or some other tool, you know how twisted the vocabulary can become as these large systems vendors try to be all things to all people. My particular pet peeve is the word "plant." In a consumer packaged goods company based in the U.S., a plant is the place where products are manufactured. Warehouses, distribution centers, sales offices, cross-docks, and other such facilities are not plants. Plants are where you make finished goods from raw materials. Unfortunately, in SAP "plant" is more akin to the meaning used by facilities managers. SAP says that a warehouse is a "plant," as are many other physical locations. While we move through a slow but steady deployment of this technology around the world, I regularly overhear co-workers trying to explain that in SAP a "plant" is not just a "plant." This often takes 30 minutes of laborious explanation before the party on the other end of the phone understands it is just a terminology problem and not some idiot from corporate who thinks a warehouse is a plant.

3. Go easy; sometimes the truth hurts

Finally, be careful how you communicate the truth. Sometimes the facts can be painful to one party or another. Even with good intention, it is prudent to be cautious with data and interpretation that will be difficult to receive. One of the errors I most regret in my career is an instance when I poorly delivered the facts.

I founded my first consulting firm in 1993 as a result of buying a "body shop" contractor out of a contract. I had been recruited several months earlier to work with a client who was quite happy with my work, but disappointed in its relationship with the contractor. When the client decided it had to let the contractor — and, therefore, me — go, I offered an alternative and bought the contract. At the moment I wrote the check, my consulting company was me and one customer. As I grew both my company and our customer base, my first customer regularly requested our services. We had a great relationship and this client was an excellent customer. Because this customer essentially started me on the road to entrepreneurship, I enjoyed a uniquely warm friendship and camaraderie with several of its associates.

It all changed when I was asked to do an assessment on a project for its sales support teams. What the client wanted to do was unique, challenging, and potentially very profitable. One of my most senior consultants and I spent several weeks honing the business case and developing a workable architecture. When we finished, we did a joint presentation with the business team to the senior decision makers. The presentation included a review of the risk matrix (chapter 8).

We did a completely honest appraisal of the project risks, one of which expressed concern that the IT department had neither the experience nor discipline to undertake a project that required the amount of finesse necessary for success on this project. Although our intention was to be informative and open, the result was that we never worked for that client again. (Guess which department hired IT consultants.) After many months of trying to correct this error in data delivery, we realized that the client was lost forever and we instituted a new tool.

Tool: Internal Business Purpose and Internal Risk Matrix

I learned the hard way that two of our tools — the business purpose and the risk matrix — each require two levels of transparency. The business purpose I described in chapter 5 and the risk matrix described in chapter 8 are both what we consider the external or outward-facing tools. On many projects, you may also keep a more private version of these tools, communicating reality only to those who need to know that aspect of reality. The use of the tools is exactly the same, but the internal versions should list things like hidden agendas, politics, and risks or purposes that are best kept private. This is also a good place to keep information that is a trade secret or confidential information about employees, customers, or partners.

Having worked in the spy business, I am cognizant of the sensitivity of different material, but most people do not have my experience and confidential material is often unmarked or treated casually. If you create two versions of a risk matrix or business purpose it is easier to make clear that one is to be kept inside the project team and not shared with others.

The relationship with my first consulting client might have been salvaged if we had built an internal risk matrix that included items like the IT department capability. This would let the client evaluate the project without regard to whom would do the work, and my team could decide how to mitigate or avoid the IT department risk separately. Russ, on the other hand, had far greater success with one of his clients.

The Real Reason We Are Doing this Project ...

Russ writes: One of my most significant project-management revelations occurred on a project I managed that involved designing, developing, and implementing an extranet system that would let a large company exchange information with literally hundreds of other companies it worked with around the country. The lifecycle of the project spanned about eight months, and we were fortunate to be working on the customer side with a great group of folks who had pretty clear ideas about what they needed and how it should work.

We gathered requirements information, created a design that included a low-fidelity prototype of the user interface (see appendix A for more on low-fidelity prototypes) and met with the project sponsor to review our results and get approval to proceed with development. The sponsor approved our approach, so we started going over the development schedule. It was then that the sponsor asked us the question every customer asks: "When can we see it?" I showed him the areas of the project plan where the user interface was going to be developed and the approximate dates.

Looking at the dates, he mentioned that the annual board meeting was coming up in a few months and that he would like to be able to "present something" during the meeting to show our progress on the project. Not thinking too much of it, I told him we should discuss it again closer to the date of the meeting so we could see where we were and what could be shown. My thought at the time was that we could show whatever pieces of the UI were most complete, and slide-ware our way through anything else that was not.

A few weeks later, during one of our weekly status meetings, he again brought up the subject of the board meeting and what we would be able to show in that timeframe. I reiterated the project plan and described what parts of the UI we were scheduled to have done by then and my plan to show these elements. He said "OK", but I was beginning to get the impression I was missing something. Luckily, we were due to be on-site again in a couple of weeks, and I resolved to ferret out whatever it was when I was there.

We arrived onsite and spent the day talking to various people. When I finally got some one-on-one time with the sponsor, I was not surprised when one of the first subjects he brought up was the board meeting. Rather than reiterating for the third time the approach we intended to take, I instead asked the question I had been waiting all day to ask: "Can you tell me a little bit more about this board meeting?"

This was when the revelation occurred. The sponsor explained to me that he had been positioning himself for a large-scale promotion that would include relocating to a different department and part of the country. He was planning to use this meeting as the forum to demonstrate to the board why he was perfect for the position. Most importantly, a big part of his push was that he had the strategic vision to sponsor the innovative project we were working on, which was not only going to save the company a significant amount of money, but was also going to demonstrate the company's leadership in its field.

Suddenly, I was seeing the board meeting in a whole new light. We could implement the best solution in the world at the end of the project, but if we didn't give the sponsor what he needed for his demo, it would fail because it wouldn't meet his objectives. To meet our sponsor's goals for the meeting, we had to have a 100-percent working user interface that he personally could demonstrate during the meeting without any direct assistance from us. As a result of understanding what success really looked like, I completely re-worked the remainder of the project plan. This included moving tasks, testing, and resources so the UI would be done and tested before the board meeting. We also scheduled extra resources to help the sponsor test and walkthrough the demo until he was completely comfortable with it. We even scheduled two "handlers" (myself and a developer) to be onsite the day before and day of the meeting to make sure everything worked as intended.

As our work to prepare the application for the meeting continued, and I patted myself on the back for discovering and reacting correctly to an important milestone, something else started to bother me. What would happen when our sponsor got his promotion and left? As with any first project for a new customer, we were hoping that it would evolve into a long-term relationship. The sponsor had apparently gone out on a limb and assumed some personal risk to get this project approved. If he suddenly dropped out of the picture before we were even finished, what would happen to the project? The momentum of the project could wither or die before it was ever completed. Now I had a new project risk that I had to find some way to mitigate.

Meanwhile, the big day came, and everything went perfectly. The sponsor was very happy with the UI and demonstrated it flawlessly to the board. That evening over dinner he told me that it couldn't have gone any better and that he was pretty confident about the promotion. That's when I brought up my concerns about what would happen to the project after he left. He admitted that he hadn't really thought about it, but now that he was aware of my legitimate concern, he would make sure the pieces were in place to ensure the project would continue to completion after he left.

He did get his promotion shortly afterward, and we implemented the project after his departure. Although the project was considered a universal success, the implementation was almost anticlimactic. It was really an eye-opening experience to see how much the interest and excitement surrounding the project waned once the board meeting had passed and our sponsor was no longer directly involved. However, the project endured, and I believe some highly evolved version of it is still in use today.

> **Take a moment to think about the biggest project on which you are currently working. It doesn't have to be an IT project. Now, complete this sentence: "This project will be successful if …"**

Now that you've read my story, take a moment to think about the biggest project on which you are currently working. It doesn't have to be an IT project. Now, complete this sentence:

"This project will be successful if …"

Were you able to come up with a simple answer quickly? Sometimes it can be more than one answer, and sometimes the answer has nothing to do with the "official" reasons for the project. It amazes me how many times I have asked someone this question about the most important project they are working on, and they don't have an answer in mind. How can you possibly be successful when you don't know what success really means?

Successful Communication

Developing both internal and external business purposes and/or risk matrices gives you insight into aspects of the project you may not have considered. But knowing and communicating are two different things. Projects that succeed follow a few simple rules for communication:

1. All critical communication, agreements, instructions, status, and results are in writing. If an agreement or important decision is made during a face-to-face meeting, one of the attendees drafts a written version of the agreement and solicits confirmations from the other participants.

2. All communication is understandable by an outsider. Acronyms are defined. Ambiguous words are avoided or clarified. Documents with business lingo include dictionaries.

3. Assertions and opinions are supported by facts, wherever possible. Opinion and interpretation are clearly indicated so they are not confused with the data.

4. Assertions and assumptions are tested and verified. Just because someone says it is so, doesn't make it so. Trust but verify.

Don't forget, when applying these rules, you must also balance transparency with appropriateness, taking advantage of the internal business purpose and risk matrix as necessary.

Chapter 13: A Hero Behind Every Tree

Those who fail to manage the first nine issues are usually counting on a hero. As we described in chapter 1, a hero is someone who can fix any problem, no matter what the circumstances, no matter what it takes, and is usually operating in permanent crisis-mode. Many companies have developed a culture of hero worship and considerable folklore around acts of heroism. I have worked with multi-billion dollar companies whose IT project plans are designed with the expectation of heroism.

As the next generation of workers enters and moves through the organization, they bring a different idea of work-life balance to the workplace. They are willing to sacrifice other compensation to get it. It becomes increasingly difficult to buy heroism.

Although you might have solved many IT problems through heroism, heroes themselves are becoming rare. As the next generation of workers enters and moves through the organization, they bring a different idea of work-life balance to the workplace. They are looking for more flexibility and more time to do the things they want to do. They are willing to sacrifice other compensation to get it.

It's becoming increasingly difficult to buy heroism. It used to be true that with a 50-percent increase in compensation you could get an employee to work like two people (a nice savings for the company) but the next generation of workers has watched the death of loyalty between company and employee in their parents and even grandparents. They have witnessed the high cost of overwork, and compensation is no longer a sufficient motivator. If they want to be a hero, they will do it in cyberspace using new tools to build communities and trade their talents. This leaves older heroes to take up the slack, but eventually even they tire of the grind and retire, leaving a heroism void.

In the U.S., we've begun importing heroes. Young Indian and Chinese IT professionals looking to make their mark are more willing to suffer the long hours and high stress that accompany heroism. This requires a constant influx of fresh heroes, because it doesn't take long for them to become frustrated with the high cost of heroism. Those organizations caught in hero syndrome will find a steady stream of candidates waiting to save them from disaster, if they can only get enough work visas.

In comic books, the heroes enter to save a city or the world from a villain. There's no villain on your project unless it is you. If you are relying on a hero, you are discarding discipline and focus for an easy escape through your IT hero — even if that hero is you. You are the evil genius who plans to conquer the IT project world, except for the fatal flaw that you're not such a genius. The cost of heroism is high. The more we rely on heroes, the more it encourages a lack of discipline in others. The entire team produces less and less, and becomes capable of less and less.

Heroism frequently involves collateral damage, such as sidestepped compliance requirements and short-sighted decision making. When the hero establishes an unrealistic pattern of work, others are encouraged to ignore other parts of their lives and concentrate on work. Heroes may salvage a project or two, but in the end everyone loses. If you are to have sustainable results, you have to work heroism out of your project and not into it.

How do you know if you are caught in the hero syndrome? The easiest measure is your concept of the work day. Twenty-four hours is not a work day and twelve hours is not a half-day. If your risk management plan, or lack thereof, depends on a surge of effort that exceeds reasonable work hours, take caution. This is a sign of hero syndrome. Remember that all work and no play makes Jack move to another company. Heroes have a tendency to move on, and over-working the rest of your staff is one of the best ways to ensure their resumes are up-to-date.

Also, remember that, no matter how hard you paddle, if you are going upstream you will never reach the ocean. The combination of solving the wrong problem (chapter 5) and using the wrong people (chapter 6) is a sign you may have a pattern of counting on hero-ism to compensate for other problems. In fact, if you are having trouble with many of the other nine issues, it is likely your project suffers from hero syndrome. If you don't see this in your organiza-tion, beware — you may be the hero.

The Dark Side of Heroism

Russ writes: There are some people who actively look to stay in the role of "hero," and it isn't simply to bask in the glory and soak up the praise. We call these guys the firefighters. The firefighter is the guy who always seems to be available and in exactly the right place to jump in and handle a crisis when it arises. Almost para-doxically, these folks are often some of the brightest and quickest thinking people in your typical resource pool, and once you see some of the reasons, you might realize why.

Based on our experience, there are a number of more subtle rea-sons, over and above the normal glory and adrenaline rush, why someone would choose to be a firefighter. To be honest, I'm guilty of succumbing to each one of these siren songs at some point in my career.

1. Clarity of purpose

Nothing makes an objective both clearer and more singular than a true crisis. You MUST drop EVERYTHING ELSE and deal with the crisis. There's no need to prioritize, no need to weigh Manager A's request against Supervisor B's, and no wondering whether it's more important to read those 300 emails or close those 300 task tickets. You have one and only one job at hand until further notice, and that is to fight the fire! I don't know how many times I've caught myself wasting time just trying to figure out what I'm supposed to be doing or, worse yet, procrastinating on some task because I'm not exactly clear what it is I'm supposed to do. I even have a phrase for it. If I'm not progressing on a task because I haven't been able to reduce it to a black-and-white "do this to achieve that," I say I'm "in the gray." If I'm wasting time flip-flopping among too many tasks and not getting anywhere on any of them, then I'm "thrashing" (and old computer term). A crisis eliminates both of these time-sinks. Fight the fire, because nothing else is as important.

2. Situational authority

I am a person who becomes particularly frustrated with having to wait for "authorization" in order to make some decision, purchase some piece of equipment, or hire some resource when I simply know that taking that action is the best way to accomplish some goal. A crisis makes all that waiting go away. For example, let's say I need to buy some piece of equipment.

On a normal project ...

> **Issue:** *The equipment we have is not adequate for the project on which I'm working.*

> **Response:** *Let's have some meetings to discuss the specs and review our budget. We present*

the request to Accounting, the IT review board approves it, and we buy the equipment, shipped ground-freight to save money, of course.

In a crisis …

Issue: *The power surge completely destroyed the box on which we've been running our mission critical legacy application.*

Response: *Call a hardware distributor and order whatever we need. Tell them to overnight it.*

3. Defer the "busy work"

This one may well be the most dangerous aspect of the firefighting hero. A crisis is the perfect chance to say, "Forget all that crap, we don't have time!!" Hardware can be added or swapped without updating support documentation. Configuration changes can be made with the entire change-management process sidestepped. Audit logs don't get filled in and compliance rules can be overlooked. All this can be done because you're in a crisis, and you can worry about that stuff later.

The danger here is twofold. At best, you end up with a backlog of this kind of detailed, but necessary, work. It's incredibly easy for everyone involved to underestimate how much effort it will take to backfill. At worst, the deferred work never gets done, which leaves the organization dangerously exposed to risks such as audits and compliance violations.

4. Escapism

Oh, how exciting it is to be a firefighter! It sure beats my normal mundane existence as a (fill in any job title here). I've seen good people literally going out of their way to look for some fire they can fight, just to escape the boring monotony of their normal day *job. Not only that, but you're actually praised and rewarded for not doing your job! And, although I can't be sure, I suspect there are times when firefighting is a more appealing alternative than whatever personal life they are setting aside.*

Tackling Heroism Head On

Unfortunately, hero syndrome is so ingrained in our thinking and culture that it is devilishly difficult to eradicate from our IT projects. Rewarding heroes extends well beyond IT projects. Most corporate folklore is built on the heroes that built the company or saved it from disaster at one point or another. In our years of encountering IT project hero syndrome, we have not found a simple, effective cure. Working on the other nine issues helps lessen the need for heroes, but it doesn't change the way we think about heroism. But, our lack of complete success in eliminating hero syndrome will not prevent us from dispensing advice. We are, after all, consultants. Where would we be if we couldn't come up with some sage wisdom for every situation?

Here, then are a few tips you can try. Although we don't have the same confidence in these as we do in our other tools, we have seen some movement away from hero syndrome when we have put these guidelines into practice.

> *Heroes tend to work their way into meetings. You'll find them in all of the planning, design, analysis, and project-review meetings. They are looking for an opportunity to step into a nearby phone booth, don their cape and tights, and swoop in to save the day.*

Meetings

Meetings are notorious time wasters. Current literature abounds with books that can help you develop better meetings. I won't steal their thunder with tips on how to have a better meeting. Instead, I want you to observe the meeting participants. Heroes tend to work their way into meetings. They may skip the training meeting covering how to use the new self-help, online benefits tool, but you'll find them in all of the planning, design, analysis, and project-review meetings. They are looking for an opportunity to step into a nearby phone booth, don their cape and tights, and swoop in to save the day. Heroes like to stay informed and, even if they are not a key participant, you'll find them haunting project meetings whether they have something to contribute or not.

Correspondingly, heroes tend to have an impressive general knowledge of the project and are welcomed into meetings because they provide bits of critical information. If you find your project team requiring Janis at every meeting because she is a "key contributor," check to be sure that Janis isn't setting herself up to be a hero. If general project knowledge is isolated to a few team members' heads, it is time to get that information out into the open.

If you observe this behavior in your project, examine the previous nine issues to see if something else is prompting heroic tendencies and correct that problem. If you just have a hero on your team, ask them to leave meetings where they really are unnecessary. When you find out they worked late to deliver something, ask if there is something you can do to help them get their work done during the work day. If everyone else can do their work as scheduled, why can't you? Their answer may provide you with some interesting insight, but more than likely they will just try to turn the question into praise of their heroic act. If your tone, body language, and words express disappointment with their heroism, over time the message will get through.

The Boss goes home

Sometimes the workday is more than eight hours. I spent over ten years in the U.S. Army and Army Reserves. I rarely worked an eight-hour day. Nonetheless, in the well-run organizations I've seen, everyone on the team has a reasonable expectation of what the work day was and can operate accordingly. The same was true in my start-up companies. The work was hard and the days were long, but they were not 24 hour days. If the organization works 14 hours a day, and that is the standard, then fine. However, if your team is putting in more hours than typical for your business, or if some team members are working significantly longer than others, you have signs of hero syndrome. One way to help reverse this trend is to ensure that the boss goes home on time. If you are the boss, don't arrive early and don't leave late. Most of all, don't acknowledge those who do.

If you keep strict hours, you won't be there to see those who are arriving early or working late, so they can't impress you by their presence. This helps, but when you go home, you need to leave work behind. This means no opening of the laptop at home, or checking messages on your handheld device. If you are an incurable workaholic, work all you want. Don't, however, include anyone else in that work. This means you can respond to all of the emails and messages you like, but you can't transmit those responses until you arrive at work (on time) in the morning. Don't call your team members for a status check. Don't respond to anyone who is operating outside of the usual and customary corporate schedule.

Your team may work on a flexible schedule or across time zones requiring routine work outside of "normal" hours. In this case, publish "boss office hours," which are those hours you work, and encourage the rest of the team to publish theirs as well. Then do not respond to or request a response from anyone outside your office hours. Expect them to do the same, making sure they work within their office hours. As with over-attendance at meetings, if you praise and reward those team members who can keep their work time within bounds while delivering quality work on time, the heroes will get the message.

Root-cause analysis

Despite your best efforts, you may have to ask for heroic effort from your team. Changing behavior takes time and some of the issues we have described may still plague your project. If you are watching for hero syndrome, you will know when someone or some group has gone above and beyond (usually to make up for an error of some kind). When this happens, gather the team and explain that the goal is to eradicate heroism and make consistent results the norm. To do that you — and by this I mean the whole group — need to determine what error set up conditions that required heroism.

The five why's of root-cause analysis will serve you well here. If you have a team tasked with, or good at, root-cause analysis ask for their help. If not, simply ask why five times. Israel and Usha worked over the weekend for the last three weeks. Why? They had to finish the Workzalot module and didn't have enough time during the week. Why? The Khambafore module was delivered late. Why? It took longer than we expected. Why? We didn't have enough experience to accurately estimate the effort and we didn't develop a risk plan to mitigate the possible results of our inexperience. Why? We haven't been updating the risk matrix as we re-estimate our projects. Root cause: poor risk-management practices, specifically managing changing risks over time.

However you do root-cause analysis, the fact that you identify heroism as aberrant behavior sends an important message to the team. The analysis and subsequent action — don't just do the analysis and take no action — further supports your message. Reinforcing a position against heroism is the fact that you saw what was happening, identified it as undesirable, and gathered the team to learn why. Eliminating endemic heroism is a long battle and will require you to prepare for and execute root-cause analysis numerous times in your project. Be sure you have appropriately budgeted for the time and effort it will take, and you will find that the reward is a smoother and more accurate project plan in the future.

Writing Heroism Out of the Project

Something I've never done, but would love to try, is to contract heroism out of the project. By this I mean I would set up the vendor agreements, team work standards, guidelines, and project governance such that heroism is strongly discouraged. To try this, I need an IT project big enough to be at risk of failure and small enough that, if this is a stupid idea, the project team can recover from the stupidity and still deliver. I'm on the prowl for such a project, but I want you to understand I have never tried this on an actual living project (laboratory rat projects do not count).

Here's how I would structure the agreements. First, a risk matrix would be part of any statement of work. Contractors, partners, and associates would be required to regularly review and update the risk matrix as part of the project. The team would then agree on the mitigation and avoidance steps and write them into the project plan. Any necessary agreements would be updated to reflect work considered acceptable if a risk occurred. The project would carry a small — very small, perhaps 1 or 2 percent — unplanned risk cushion. The team would respond to planned risks as per the risk-management plan. These actions would be clearly communicated as planned responses to known risks and not heroism. The people who would be thanked would be those with the foresight to identify and plan for the risk. The people executing the mitigation plan would just be following work instructions as with any routine project work.

When unplanned risks occur, the people affected would be given the option to use their portion of the small risk cushion, or to mitigate the risk at their expense. I'm not sure exactly how this might work, except that the goal of this rule would be to make unplanned risk mitigation clearly the consequences of poor planning rather than heroism. This might mean that team members would sometimes pay for the poor planning of their managers. To avoid this, the team members should participate in risk planning and sign off on the risk matrix. The agreement must also cause risk planners to be penalized for missed risks in the form of reduction in bonuses or other compensation, without affecting the team that has to make up for the poor plan. If an unplanned risk causes the team to miss a key project milestone, the team members who should suffer most from the missed milestone are the risk planners.

I would add a requirement that the budget for hours worked be strictly adhered to. Team members caught putting in extra hours would suffer a penalty and vendors paying contractors for hours beyond those in the project plan would suffer a two-for-one penalty, losing two hours of compensation for every one hour worked outside of the plan. Like the risk plan, both the management team and the individual contributors would need to sign off on the agreements. The cost of errors in judgment would be not only unpaid hours, but also an additional penalty of some kind.

Frankly, I don't know if something like this could ever work, but if it could, we would forever think about heroism in a different light. Getting our focus on discipline and truly thinking smarter rather than harder would be more beneficial than having a hero in reserve. One measure of how disciplined your IT team is, is their willingness to take on some or all of these suggestions for writing heroism out of their next IT project.

> *Unfortunately, simply plugging project heroes into more consistent, evenly paced work doesn't always work. If they miss the adrenaline and high stress of firefighting, they'll either start looking for smoke somewhere else ... or create their own!*

Hero vaccine

Russ writes: As I discussed in the section titled The Dark Side of Heroism, sometimes people are heroes not only because the project/environment dictates it, but simply because they want to be. So, if your plan is to eliminate the need for heroism in your environment, then you'll also need to identify those that might not like the idea and consider how much of an impact it will have on them. Unfortunately, simply plugging these people into more consistent, evenly paced work doesn't always work. If they miss the adrenaline and high stress of firefighting, they'll either start looking for smoke somewhere else … or create their own!

Here are some suggestions for how to keep these kinds of people happy:

1. Throw them the stickiest wickets

Heroes that are also good at what they do are usually fantastic candidates for tackling the most challenging requirements and/or aspects of an IT project. Feeding your hero a steady diet of complex problems that must be solved is a great way to keep them engaged. If you can, allow them a certain amount of "situational authority" in order to accomplish their tasks.

2. Allow a flexible schedule

I learned this one a long time ago from a contractor, whom I'll call John, I had working for me on a development project. At the beginning of each week, I would sit down with the development team, and go over what I expected each person to have done by the end of the week.

Over the course of the week, I would check in with each developer to chat and see how they were doing. I noticed that John stayed late on one particular Monday and Tuesday. Then, on a Wednesday, I stopped by John's desk, only to find him playing an online computer game. Of course, my first reaction was, "What are you doing when you should be working on the purchasing module?" His reply was "I'm finished." So, we reviewed his work and he in fact had successfully finished everything I had asked him to do. After some more discussion with him, we agreed that as long as he got everything done that I needed him to do, he was free to indulge in the occasional distraction. But I also asked him to give me the courtesy of letting me know when he had finished his week's work.

The point here is that John was doing exactly what I needed him to do, within the timeframe I needed him to do it. He wanted to put in a super-human effort at the beginning of the week so he could slack off at the end. Since, in this case, there was no risk in allowing this, I decided there was no reason to penalize him for it.

> **Allowing someone to slack off in the first part of the week, with the anticipation of applying heroics at the end, is dangerous.**

However, be aware that there is almost always risk in allowing the opposite to happen. Allowing someone to slack off in the first part of the week, with the anticipation of applying heroics at the end, is dangerous. There's a risk they find out on Thursday that they really did need to work on their project Monday through Wednesday.

3. Manufacture stress

I almost decided not to include this one, but I've used it successfully too many times (usually on myself) not to share it. The simple reality is that some people work better when they are under a certain amount of stress, and they will actually perform better and more happily at a certain level of stress that may not exist in a de-heroed environment. For these types of people, I recommend setting goals that exceed the requirements of the project. For example, if a particular task is required to be completed in three weeks, then insist on them delivering it in two. Follow up with them regularly to reinforce this goal as a real objective. This is also a great way to manage risk, because you are building in extra time on each task to deal with unforeseen issues.

If the timeline isn't conducive to this type of approach, find ways to encourage them exceed the requirements of whatever task(s) they've been given. However, this kind of approach needs to be closely managed, because you want to make sure the base requirements are still met within the timeline and using only the resources allowed. Put another way, don't employ this strategy if it's going to cause cost overruns, or cause your resource to deliver late.

Chapter 14: Taking Action

A voiding the ten issues we've described in this book is simple; yet so few people responsible for IT projects do. Our advice falls into these easy rules:

- Trust but verify
- Solve the right problem, define success
- Collect the facts, then face them
- Manage your risks
- Communicate well
- Keep in shape
- Discipline, discipline, discipline

Perhaps I should restate. Avoiding these ten issues is simple — conceptually. The challenge is in the doing, and that is clearly not so easy. In this chapter we will address action. One of the reasons Russ and I make a good team is that I've always found it easier to dream up a solution than to implement it, and Russ has always found it easier to implement a solution than to dream it up. This doesn't mean that Russ never invents and I never implement, but our natural preferences go the other way.

> **Avoiding these ten issues is simple — conceptually. The challenge is in the doing, and that is clearly not so easy.**

From Magic to Repeatable Process

Russ and I met in the early 1990s, but never expected to work under the same management together. However, after a start-up I helped found failed to get next-round funding just prior to the dot-com crash (lucky for those would-be investors), Russ' boss rescued me from wandering aimlessly as an independent consultant and I joined Russ' team for about a year. One of the main reasons I was hired onto the team was to transfer the techniques I had been using for fixed-price custom software development to Russ' team. He had an excellent consulting group made up of mostly junior and mid-level consultants who had the potential to be mid-level and senior consultants with the right tutelage and techniques.

On our first job together, I got out my favorite whiteboard pen and started drawing diagrams. I had explained some of the things I would accomplish on our first day with the client and Russ patiently watched while I danced around the whiteboards. At the end of the day he was full of questions. Why did I switch from one diagram to another? Which diagram should come first? Why was the business purpose intentionally brief? To me, he sounded like a five-year-old desperate to know everything, now. My explanation was that it was magic. I just felt my way through it and came up with the right answers. I believe his exact words were, "You're full of crap."

He went on to convince me that I acted in a logical and rational pattern. His job was to get that pattern out of my head and onto paper so we could train the other consultants, as well as improve and refine the techniques. As it turned out, I was full of crap and we did document the techniques. We found that the techniques I had been using appeared to form a pattern that looked remarkably like the Zachman Framework (we used this in chapter 10 to deal with second-order ignorance). When we placed my tools inside the framework, we found gaps that fit exactly where we had been uncomfortable in our project work thus far.

From that point, we set out to both train others in the techniques and to fill the gaps in the framework. Some of the tools in the preceding chapters are the result of that work and some existed before we put them into John Zachman's framework. We have used this framework primarily as a tool for software development projects. It is a particularly good collection of tools for discovery, design, testing, review, and negotiation when you must capture and fulfill the correct business requirements in order to build something new to achieve expected results. We have used the framework in one form or another for other kinds of IT investments, and have used the individual tools as needed to combat hero syndrome and the other non-technical issues we have discussed in this book.

I'm going to explain how we use the framework, and a little bit about its contents to give you a context for where the tools we've already described fit. I will then recap the tools we believe will help you address these top ten non-technical issues and achieve project success.

Insight Anthology

Because we are consultants, the collection of tools has a name. We call it Insight Anthology™. Just because it has a cool trademark, doesn't make it anything special. Most of these tools are adapted from the ideas of other much smarter people. You can find some their original works in the bibliography. All we've done is take a lot of complicated material and put it into a memorable framework (thanks to John Zachman). It is very likely that you have developed some of your own tools and techniques that serve you well. We encourage you to add your tools to the toolkit (discarding ours if they don't suit your purposes). The whole idea is to give you a toolkit with which you can manage the risks posed by the non-technical issues we have raised.

> Insight Anthology is the systematic application of techniques that, when taken as a whole, yields the knowledge and understanding that allows you to predict project outcomes.

If you believe this description, I suggest you re-read chapter 4.

	What	How	Where	Who	When	Why
Scope (Idea)	Business Purpose	Business Purpose	Business Purpose	Business Purpose	Business Purpose	Business Purpose
Context (Proposal)	Context Model	Process Model	Context Map	Work Relationship Diagram	Benefits Over Time	Benefits Over Time
Logical (Req./ PMP)	Class/Data & Component Model	Essential Use Case	Technology Map	User Roles	Architectural Milestones	Benefits Over Time
Physical (Design)	Low-Fidelity Prototype	LFP & Interface Spec.	Network Map	Use Case to LFP Map & Security Rules	Success Metrics	Success Metrics with ROI
Construct (Develop)	Hardware, Software, Database	Software Config.	Network Deployment Plan	People & Security Access List	Calendar, Project & Deployment Plan	Marketing Bulletin & Benefits

Figure 7: The Insight Anthology tools in the Zachman framework

Using the Framework

What we really do is take tools that work for us and place them in the Zachman Framework. The current set of tools is listed in Figure 7. If you look at the version of the Zachman Framework on www. zifa.org you will find the tools in the cells to be somewhat different. Just to be clear, Zachman's philosophy is to look at the architecture of the enterprise (which requires a purer set of models). Our approach is to successfully complete individual IT projects. Thus, we twist the content to our own purposes to have a quick-and-dirty tool-kit that can be used after a five-minute explanation using a pencil and paper.

In each of the cells, we want to answer the question (who, what, when, where, why, how) in the context of the row (idea, proposal, requirements, design, developed product). The tools we choose specifically fit their cell (or, in some cases, multiple cells). They work well to manage second-order ignorance (chapter 10) on a cell-by-cell basis and work together to give a picture of the IT project as a whole. In addition to the tools in the framework, we use a few that stand alone to address the project as a whole. In the case of managing second-order ignorance, we use the framework itself as a tool.

In the rest of the chapter I will fit the tools we described in individual chapters where they belong in the framework to show you what we have addressed. Then, I will recap the tools that reside outside the framework. The appendix has a brief description of the tools not covered in the preceding chapters to satiate the curious.

Business Purpose

Since all of the really important mistakes on a project are made the first day, the first place of focus is the business purpose. The business purpose prevents you from solving the wrong problem (chapter 5) and helps you communicate reality rather than giving perception sway (chapter 12). By using an internal business purpose, you can communicate those things to the project team that are true, but aren't polite or politically correct to air in public. Combined, the business purposes cover the entire first row of the matrix answering who, what, when, where, why, and how. We provided an example of a business purpose document in chapter 5. The business purpose should be limited to one page. It should be concise but complete, and answer all the interrogatives. Most importantly, it must answer the question why.

> *Since all of the really important mistakes on a project are made the first day, the first place of focus is the business purpose.*

To call your project a success, you must be able to prove that you achieved the objective. To do that, the objective must be clear before you even begin. Remember that a good business purpose is clear, and vocabulary can be troublesome. Use unambiguous terms or ensure your business purpose and project dictionary are in agreement. True of all of the tools, but particularly important for a business purpose, is that it should be good enough. You are unlikely to write the perfect business purpose document, so don't even try. If you have answered all six interrogatives and spelled out why in measurable terms, then stop. You can refine as you proceed, but get something into the hands of the project team as quickly as you can. The business purpose serves as the foundation for the rest of the project. Major changes could have a negative impact, but small tweaks and refinements are natural as you understand more and more of the important details.

When you are satisfied with the external business purpose, lock it down and don't change it unless it is through a formal change-control process. It's cheating to modify the goals when you discover you can't deliver all of them. If the organization accepts that a change in outcome is still worth the investment, the organization can modify the business purpose to reflect that decision. Most important to understand is that this decision does not lie with the IT group or project team. It must come from the steering committee or executive leadership making the investment.

Remember that an internal business purpose is exactly the same in structure as an external one, except it is not to be shared outside of the project team. It is used to hold answers to the interrogatives — again particularly the question why — that are best kept quiet. Should you fail to understand the internal business purpose, your project success is in the same jeopardy as it would be without a well-written external business purpose. Some projects don't require an internal business purpose because hidden agendas and parallel goals don't exist. But, in those cases where these elements do exist, an internal business purpose is invaluable.

To make it easier on the reader, we sometimes include the entire business purpose in the internal version — including the full contents of the external business purpose in addition to the internal content. Use care with this technique as it makes the internal information more likely to be inadvertently shared. If the internal purpose is highly sensitive or strictly confidential then do not mix the content.

Benefits over Time

The next three tools — the benefits-over-time document, architectural milestones, and success metrics — all come from chapter 7 and relate to measurement. They all relate to the question "why." If you are focused on the delivery of business value for your IT investments, your measurements should point you toward delivering on those promises. If you promised 10 percent additional sales, then measure sales. If you promised a 5-percent reduction in purchasing costs, then measure purchasing costs. If you promised to reduce headcount by 18 people, then measure headcount. These tools help you see the benefits so you can measure the right things.

The benefits-over-time document is simply a description or chart of the benefits, as found in the business purpose, mapped against fixed and variable time events. You will discover these time events when you explore the question "when." They should also be described in general terms in the business purpose. Unlike the business purpose, the benefits-over-time document should explain the context of your work. A well-reasoned benefits-over-time document is the foundation for justifying the IT investment. It is an explanation of the return your investment should yield and the timeframe in which it matures (in whole or in part).

In addition to serving as part of the investment justification, a good benefits-over-time document begins to set the project schedule. The IT project manager should be using the benefits-over-time document to make key decisions that maximize the returns as early as possible. Money, time, and resources returned to the organization can be spent on other things. The sooner you can free them to be used by the organization the more valuable the project is overall.

Architectural Milestones

The next step in connecting why and when is to create benefits milestones on a project plan, usually in the form of a Gantt chart. After the basic benefits-over-time data has been transferred to a project plan, the project manager can then connect critical steps in the project and necessary deliverables to those benefits milestones.

Chapter 7 has an example, but the important thing to note is that the milestones are not activities, but benefits. Based on the project plan, the team should know what benefits accrue as a result of their work. You might see several tasks that lead to a benefit milestone, but you shouldn't see any milestones that don't accrue some benefit.

You should watch projects that have a very long timeline before any benefits accrue. A plan for this kind of project should include one or more decision points for further investment. For example, I worked on a project with an almost two-year benefits cycle. For a variety of legitimate reasons, the time between the first dollar invested and the first dollar harvested was a minimum of twenty months.

To make that timespan more palatable for the investors, we segmented the project into three chunks. The first phase would prove the capabilities of the system and identify the hardware necessary to run it. We invested about 25 percent of the total project budget and on a particular date delivered a firm estimate of the hardware and licensing costs and a reassessment of the benefits that would be provided. Although 25 percent of the project was sunk at that point, the benefit was that 75 percent of the investment could be salvaged if it appeared necessary at that point.

The project had two other go/no-go stages on a fixed calendar. These stages corresponded with business decision making so, if the investment was canceled, the monies reserved but not yet spent could be quickly directed to another investment. Good architectural milestones directly connect concrete project work directly connected to fixed or even variable benefits on a timeline.

Success Metrics

Also described in chapter 7, success metrics are a method of communicating project status to those not intimately involved in the details of the project. We usually present this as a dashboard, but sometimes this information can be conveyed in a simple grid on a sheet of paper with summary information on it. The key to a success metrics dashboard is to focus again on the benefits. Why are we doing this? What must we accomplish to get there? What are the drivers of success and where do they stand? These are the questions answered by a success metrics dashboard. Using the architectural milestones and key steps to achieve them, you simply create a list

U-catchem Project Success Metrics Dashboard as of July				
	date	measure	value	measurement
Design/Blueprint				
business purpose	July	document approved	pass	pass/fail
benefits over time	July	document approved	pass	pass/fail
architectural milestones	July	Gantt chart approved	pass	pass/fail
system design	August	design submitted for test		pass/fail
design acceptance test	August	revised design tested and accepted		pass/fail
project review stage gate	September	review of investment vs. return		pass/fail
Development				
contract mgr module test	October	module test plan passed		pass/fail
month-end module test	October	module test plan passed		pass/fail
integration test	November	integration test plan passed		pass/fail

conversion test	November	conversion test plan passed		pass/fail
training plan complete	December	training materials & plan approved		pass/fail

Implementation

baseline measurement	November	baseline measurements taken	35%	weighted value of completions (of 100%)
system installation	December	installed system functional test		pass/fail
production data load & test	December	customer & integration data loaded and tested		pass/fail
salesman training begins	December	salesmen trained	0 / 236	trained / total
conversion of salesmen	January	salesmen converted to new system	0 / 236	converted / total

End Game

temp headcount reduction	begins March	reduction of 36 contractor hours/month	0	contractor hours
reduce overnight packages	begins March	total $ from $75M baseline	0	dollars saved (baseline - actual)
printer/copier retirement	begins February	incremental reduction of two machines	0	machines retired
increase in contracts	begins in May	increase from 10M contracts of between 2-5%	0	actual weekly contracts in new system - baseline weekly average contracts of converted salesmen
increase in projected revenue	begins in May	based on contract increase. Not all increases will be attributed to this project as the business is also focused on increasing revenue per contract which is unrelated to this project.	0	Contract dollar YTD vs. prior YTD

Figure 8: Success metrics dashboard example (repeated from chapter 7)

of items and dates, along with a measure of benefits achieved and accrued value to date. Russ likes to categorize them by project phase or other logical breakdown to give individual items focus around a larger event.

The format is completely up to you and many of our friends and clients use software to display and manage a dashboard on the corporate intranet site. I have included the example from chapter 7 here (Figure 8 on pages 200 and 201) because, in this case, seeing is understanding. In your success metrics you want to build something that the executive team can easily consume and understand without any explanation. They need to be able to do this in mere seconds, which is all the time your pretty chart is going to get.

Matrix Review

These four tools — the business purpose, the benefits-over-time document, architectural milestones, and success metrics — are the only tools taken directly from the Insight Anthology matrix. However, you might notice the pattern of second-order ignorance these cover. Figure 9 shows what a second-order ignorance matrix would look like if you did nothing but use the tools I just described.

	What	How	Where	Who	When	Why
Scope (Idea)						
Context (Proposal)	20	20	20	20		
Logical (Req./PMP)	15	15	15	15		
Physical (Design)	10	10	10	10		
Construct (Develop)	5	5	5	5	5	5
Total						210

Figure 9: 2OI matrix template, after using recommended tools

A fresh matrix has a score of 450 and, with these simple tools, we have reduced the risk factor by more than half.

You might also notice that these tools are heavily skewed toward strategy, when and why. The reason might not be profound, but it is important. We IT people have spent most of the history of our field developing tools to help us solve technical problems. We began by managing how. We invented flow charts, data-flow diagrams, process models, and the like. We invented procedures, structured programming, and object-oriented systems to tackle the question how. We also tackled what. We invented file structures, added indexes, developed hierarchies, and eventually created relational databases.

Not satisfied, we invented object databases and three-dimensional structures with cubes that will let business people (who are also skilled geeks) slice and dice corporate information to their hearts' content. As communication and connectivity became more important we moved to the question of where. We invented modems to capitalize on the world wide copper framework that supported telephone communications. From there, we invented local area networks, metropolitan networks, and wide area networks. Even politicians got involved. While he wasn't writing legislation, Al Gore invented the Internet and we all surfed happily on our cell phones and wireless laptops built on infrastructure designed from detailed network diagrams and other "where" tools.

Your IT people have what, how, and where down pat. Did you notice the order of the Zachman Framework? When John first published his framework it only had three columns. According to him, he envisioned the whole thing, but didn't think people would believe that who, when, and why belonged in the enterprise architecture. After all, the gurus of IT had only invented tools to address what, how, and where.

If IT people can handle the first three interrogatives, everyone else needs to have some skills with who, when, and why — and the greatest of these is why. Want to solve IT technical problems?

Concentrate on what, how, and where. Want to solve non-technical problems? Focus on who, when, and why. In the same way, the strategy row is the least technical. This is where you decide what it is all about. As you move down the levels, the information gets easier and easier to codify (until, at the bottom, it is pure code). The techies in IT are very good at codifying, classifying, diagramming, and otherwise sorting things into neat piles. Strategy is notoriously difficult to codify.

What makes these tools different from your typical self-help IT book tools is that they focus on where your IT staff is weakest.

What makes these tools different from your typical self-help IT book tools is that they focus on where your IT staff is weakest. If you want to improve your team's skills in the other columns, simply send them to training or hire people who already have those skills. When it comes to strategy — when and why — very few IT people have those skills. Developing them will require a considerable shift in thinking inside your IT department.

Project Dictionary

The next set of tools — the project dictionary, risk matrix, second-order-ignorance risk matrix, audition, and peer review — falls outside of the framework, but they are nevertheless important parts of the toolkit.

> **dic·tion·ar·y**[17]
>
> –noun, plural -ar·ies.
>
> **2.** a book giving information on particular subjects or on a particular class of words, names, or facts, usually arranged alphabetically: a biographical dictionary; a dictionary of mathematics.

[17] "Dictionary." Dictionary.com Unabridged (v 1.1). New York: Random House, 22 September 2008. <Dictionary.com>

3. Computers. a list of codes, terms, keys, etc., and their meanings, used by a computer program or system.

The most important aspect about a project dictionary is whether it is used (chapter 5). Make it relevant, usable, and easy to access. Attach it to anything where specialized terms or ambiguity could be a problem.

Risk Matrix

I hope we have convinced you that hope is not a risk management strategy (chapter 8). Given that all investments carry some risk and that IT projects are complex, resulting in a complex set of risks, managing those risks becomes extremely important. The risk matrix is a simple tool to help you manage risk quickly and effectively.

Simply brainstorm all possible risks. Give each risk a name or short description and give it two rankings: one for likelihood and one for impact using a score between 1 and 5, where 1 is unlikely or no impact and 5 is will happen or catastrophic failure. Multiply the two rankings to get a risk score. Sort risks by score and manage the top ten or so. For each risk, develop an avoidance and/or mitigation plan and adjust the overall project plan to match.

An example risk matrix looks like Figure 10

Risk	Likelihood	Impact	Score	Mitigation
Hardware not available on time	5	4	20	Request delivery guarantees when ordering equipment
Key project sponsor leaves company	3	5	15	Identify most likely successor determine project stance
Proposed technology does not work	2	4	8	Identify back-up technology/schedule

Figure 10: Risk matrix example (repeated from chapter 8)

As I discussed in chapter 12, sometimes you need two risk matrices: one that you publish and one that you keep internal to the project team. If you recall, I lost a customer after telling them in the public risk matrix that one of the top risks was the IT department's likely lack of skill for handling a project like the one we were proposing. Never lie to your customers, but if the fact that they are both stupid and ugly somehow translates to a risk in your project, you may want to keep that information to yourself. An internal risk matrix is the perfect way to do so.

> **Never lie to your customers, but if the fact that they are both stupid and ugly somehow translates to a risk in your project, you may want to keep that information to yourself.**

Second-Order Ignorance Matrix

Using the Zachman framework, we put a fence around those areas where we don't know what we don't know (the definition of second-order ignorance), but we know that we need to know if any such unknowns exist. Using the tools in this chapter and in the appendix, explore an interrogative from one perspective until you are reasonably sure you have moved all second-order ignorance to at least first-order ignorance. Anything else should be impossible to anticipate. When you have done this, remove the number from that cell and update the total. The second-order-ignorance matrix in Figure 9 shows a project where the tools described in this chapter were used. The resulting risk score is 210. Figure 6 in chapter 10 shows the entire matrix before a project begins.

Higher scores mean a higher risk of a project "gotcha" resulting from not knowing what you don't know. In our experience a score of 100 or less is a sufficiently low risk score. At this point, second-order ignorance generally falls off of the risk matrix and it is no longer important to track.

Audition

This is my favorite way of getting the right people into your organization or onto your project (chapter 6). Don't interview (not even on the telephone). Simply review their qualifications and bring in a bunch for an audition. Give them a short assignment that would be something you would expect them to handle on their first day of work. Provide them with the necessary materials and resources to do the work, and let them go do it. Rate the auditions on quality of work, fit, and any other criteria you deem important to the position. You can be as creative as you'd like, but simple usually does the trick. If you give your candidates an impossible task, both you and your candidates will be frustrated.

Bear in mind that the top movie actors are known and don't usually do auditions. Their past work serves as an audition. If you want them, call their agent and work out a deal. The same is true of IT professionals. If you want a superstar, go get one on the recommendation of their past work. Don't try to audition a superstar. Hold auditions for all of the rest of the parts you need filled.

Peer Review

Another chapter 10 tool to prevent ignorance as a defense is the peer review. Unlike typical "code reviews," a peer group should review any deliverable from the business purpose down to the database schema. The rules of a peer review are simple:

- Provide the material in advance (and reviewers should review the material in advance without distributing their comments).
- Schedule a meeting of limited duration (15-30 minutes works well).

- Have a facilitator.
- Do not allow the author to attend the review.
- Compile the comments from the meeting. The possible outcomes are:
  - Pass
  - Pass with minor corrections
  - Fail
- On either of the Pass outcomes, the review team assumes responsibility for the deliverable and the author is off-the-hook.

Select the peers to review the materials from those whose current work or previous experience makes them capable of understanding the form of the work product to be reviewed (e.g., computer language, diagram or model, design document, etc.) and whose role on the project or in the organization enables them to review the content as it applies to the business problem.

Peer reviews are a way to check for adherence to standards and required practices. If you recall, I could have programmed a back door into a critical electronic signature component of a pharmaceutical clinical trials system because nobody reviewed the work at the appropriate level of detail.

Incentives

The first tool we introduced in chapter 1 was a set of rules for incentives they are:

Rule1: Always reward success

Rule 2: Always reward discipline

Rule 3: Always reward improvement

Remember too that the incentives have to actually motivate your team members. Sometimes a simple thing like recognition for a job well done is enough, but whatever the incentive it must do its job or you should find another incentive.

Tool Rules

The only remaining tool is the set of rules for selecting tools. If you have your own tools or are evaluating some you would like to use, check them against this list:

Rule 1: Easy to use

Rule 2: Valuable

Rule 3: Easy to explain

Rule 4: Pencil and paper

Rule 5: Low fidelity

Rule 6: Iterative

Rule 7: Focus on flaws

Rule 8: Front-load risks

Rule 9: Self-testing

Rule10: Self-leveling

Rule 11: Self-documenting

And most important, not only for selecting tools but also for using them: Good enough is good enough. Perfection is not required on most projects and it is rarely required to make effective use of the tools in this chapter.

Redefining Heroism

Armed with the knowledge of what causes failure in many IT projects and with a set of tools to springboard you to success, what remains? Responsibility remains. Early in the book I told you I would be hard on the executives who decide to make IT investments and who are assigned to manage them. I have probably failed to be hard enough. The problem is responsibility. Have the courage to take responsibility for IT investments and make both the investment and return clear.

When things go wrong, have the courage to say so. The old way of reporting to the board of directors is: "You approved a $3M IT investment to build a digital rights management system. This quarter, the IT department installed the digital rights management system at a cost of $2.5M" The other departments — those whiners — complain about how broken the system is and how it doesn't deliver on its promises.

Instead say: "I took responsibility to deliver $25 million in value for a $3 million investment in a digital rights system. The system was installed this quarter but failed to meet expectations. The measured benefits, less the increased costs, make it a break-even system not including the initial investment. I believe that we can ultimately deliver $10 million in value for the remaining $.5 million and six more months of work. I have prepared a presentation on why we failed and how we plan to recover some of the return if you would like further details."

At the opening of the chapter I suggested you need only follow these simple rules:

- Trust but verify
- Solve the right problem, define success
- Collect the facts, then face them
- Manage your risks
- Communicate well
- Keep in shape
- Discipline, discipline, discipline

Take the responsibility to deliver IT project results and expect —

no, *demand* — these things from your IT staff, from your vendors, and from your consultants. Doing this puts you on a path to true heroism.

Russ writes: *At this point, we hope we've given you enough insight to know when rampant project heroism exists in your environment and what you can do to eliminate it. But how do you know when you've been successful? One word is the key: consistency. Let me elaborate:*

Consistent project progress — *Projects that don't require heroics to succeed typically exhibit a steady, even flow of progress throughout their lifecycle, instead of hitting a brick wall every time some new cataclysm strikes, and then lurching forward at a frantic pace when the hero steps in to save the day and make up the lost time. Instead, tasks are calmly completed on time and,*

> **Projects that don't require heroics to succeed typically exhibit a steady, even flow of progress throughout their lifecycle, instead of hitting a brick wall every time some new cataclysm strikes, and then lurching forward at a frantic pace when the hero steps in to save the day and make up the lost time.**

when problems do arise, one or more members of the team are prepared to resolve them immediately, without the project coming to a screeching halt.

Consistent resource scheduling — *This is one of the easiest elements to measure. If your project team is always busy, but still regularly puts in eight-hour days, five days a week and uses their vacation time, then you clearly have an environment that doesn't need heroic efforts to churn out successful projects.*

Consistent stress levels — *I've worked in the financial industry long enough to see the near-panic that can set in at the mere mention of the word "auditor," and the ensuing all-hands mad scramble to make sure the organization is prepared for the day they swoop in. That was the old days, a constant cycle of high stress, followed by gigantic sighs of relief when each audit is over.*

The organization I worked with has changed its tactics completely. It now treats audits as just another routine activity, for which there is a consistent, repeatable process in place, complete with contingency plans to deal with unforeseen gaps. Instead of relying on the heroes to deal with the auditors and save the day, the requirements the auditors look for are now part of everyone's daily routine, which means no more audit stress!

The Real IT Heroes

Russ and I have a list of people we consider the real IT heroes. These are project managers who can be absent for several weeks of illness without losing any ground, and software developers who keep their teams in shape so effective resources were always available.

Russ and I have a list of people we consider the real IT heroes. These are project managers who can be absent for several weeks of illness without losing any ground, and software developers who keep their teams in shape so effective resources were always available. Those with sufficient discipline that their children know their faces are the kinds of heroes we celebrate. Recently, I have been working with a project leader who exhibits many of these qualities, yet he still feels compelled to take work home to compensate for a team with imbalanced skills and risks that were not front-loaded. I am hopeful that this book and some mentoring will help eliminate the unhealthy heroism encouraged by his years of IT experience, and turn him toward the kind of heroism Russ and I so respect.

Russ writes: *Steve and I aren't naïve enough to insist that all heroic efforts are both unnecessary and undeserving of praise. It's inevitable that unforeseen circumstances can and will arise, and that monumental efforts by one or more individuals can make the difference between success and failure. The point is that this kind of repeated pattern of disaster and recovery is as unhealthy and unsustainable for a team and an organization as regularly gaining and losing 30 pounds.*

The "hero-syndrome" style of IT heroes won't fix things. Build a team of the right people, one that doesn't need a hero to save it and become a new kind of hero. Recently, I was sent to a difficult project in west Texas. A friend of mine, originally from that area, offered this advice, "Don't worry; there's a hero behind every tree." When I arrived, I called him back. "Hey," I said, "There are no trees!" Good thing I had learned some of these lessons already.

Appendix A

The main body of the book does not include all of the tools listed in Figure 7 (chapter 14) because many of the tools don't apply to the topic directly. This appendix provides brief descriptions of the remaining tools in the matrix, except for the bottom column. For that column, you need to take several classes leading to a degree in MIS or Computer Science. The tools covered in the appendix are:

- Context Row
    - Context Model
    - Process Model
    - Context Map
    - Work Relationship Diagram
- Logical Row
    - Class/Data Model
    - Component Model
    - Essential Use Case
    - Technology Map
    - User Roles
- Physical Row
    - Low-Fidelity Prototype

- Interface Specification
- Network Map
- Use-Case-to-LFP Map

Bear in mind that each of these tools follows the rules outlined in chapter 2. Thus, some of the example images are scanned paper-and-pencil diagrams because that is the right approach (not because we were too cheap to draw them neatly for publication).

Context Model

Answers: What and Who
Perspective: Context

If you are old enough to be familiar with data-flow diagrams, the context model is simply a zero-level data-flow diagram. The best description of these is in Essential Systems Analysis[18]. In brief it is

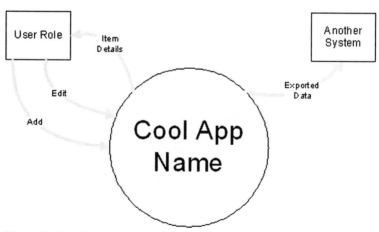

Figure 11: Drawing a context model

[18] McMenamin, Stephen M. and John F. Palmer. Essential Systems Analysis. Upper Saddle River, New Jersey: Prentice-Hall, 1984.

a big circle depicting the project. Everything inside the circle is in scope and everything on the outside is out of scope. The lines are human or system interactions directly with the system. They are in essence the user or system interfaces you will have to build. The diagram very specifically only depicts interactions with the system. Interactions between other systems or users of the systems are not modeled here. The boxes are user roles as illustrated in the user roles and the work relationship diagram sections to follow.

Using Figure 11 on the previous page as a guide, the roles should include both the people and systems that will interact with your system. The lines have direction (always in one direction; draw a

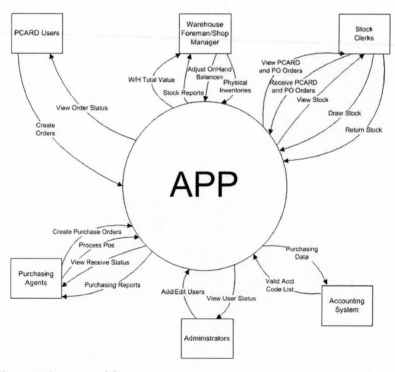

Figure 12: Context model

second line if the communications are bi-directional) and you can be as general or specific about what is on the line as necessary to get the point across. Some practice will help you judge the appropriate level of abstraction. Last, your context diagram should sport the system's name in the center. This is a good time to name your project if you haven't already.

Where a line touches the boundary of your system, you must create an interface. Thus, the context model shows some of the scope of the work necessary to provide business value. The context model makes an excellent negotiating tool when one group wants feature A and another wants feature B. Start adding lines and ask how much more they are willing to invest, or which lines they will sacrifice. It is amazing how quickly passion turns to logic when demanding people are faced with a context model. Figure 12 shows a context model from a real project.

Process Model

Answers: How (and sometimes Who and What)
Perspective: Context

Process modeling is a mature IT systems practice. We have used several different process models successfully and don't have a strong preference for one style over another. At the context level, a process model should show high-level work or process flows indicating the transformation of data or material. Each box is a step in the process and might itself be a process requiring its own model. Beware that you don't model the process to death. We have seen several IT projects die of over-analysis, due mostly to intense and unnecessary process modeling. A little goes a long way when it comes to process models.

When nobody cares, we use an IDEF0 model because it lets us depict inputs, outputs, constraints and resources. The IDEF0 model in Figure 13 is from a real project. You can easily see the inputs and outputs (some of which might cycle back through a process). The arrows pointing down into the boxes indicate resources. At several steps, input from outside resources is required and those resources are indicated on the model. Were there constraints, they would be indicated with arrows pointing up toward the bottom of the process box. A constraint would be something like the process can only run at month-end, or only between 4:00 and 5:00.

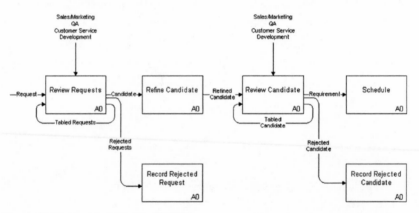

Figure 13: Process model (style: IDEF0)

Context Map

Answers: Where (and sometimes Who or What)
Perspective: Context

A context map is any appropriate generalized map that shows where the various pieces, players, and connections of your system physically reside. This diagram is meant to be the spatial context of the network or interconnections that will be required. Be sure to map both systems and user roles and identify physical locations and network connections. From project to project, we draw these in very different ways depending on the scope of "where" in the project. Sometimes you can use a building diagram and sometimes a globe is necessary. The idea at the context level is to ensure you understand the scope of location and what that means to your project. The example in Figure 14 is from a real project. At one point, this diagram averted certain disaster (a story Russ will be happy to tell you over beers).

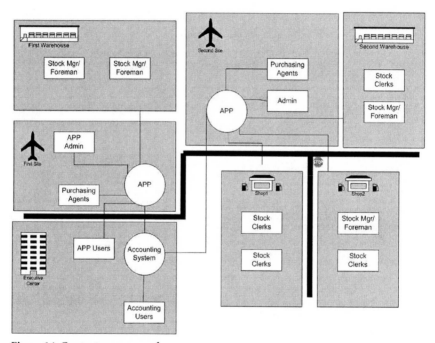

Figure 14: Context map example

Work-Relationship Diagram

Answers: Who (and a little bit of What)
Perspective: Context

A work-relationship diagram (WRD) identifies the business roles related to a system. You could conceivably create one for the whole organization, but we tend to use these only at the project level. This is a typical box-and-line diagram and is, incidentally, the only one of the box-and-line diagrams that you won't find elsewhere because we invented it. A WRD is designed to tell you what you wish you could get from an organization chart, namely what everybody really does. It is what it says it is: a diagram showing the work relationships between roles in the organization. It shows the information, goods, and services passed from one role to another.

The boxes represent roles within the organization and should directly map to the user roles as described in the following bulleted list. Some of the boxes should also appear on the context diagram if they directly interact with the system you are describing. Although some of the diagrams we describe in the appendix are strictly limited to people and things that directly interact with the system, to get a more complete picture, we prefer to extend the WRD to include more people or roles. Likely candidates for your WRD are:

- People who create things related to the system
- People who change things related to the system
- People who consume things created by the system
- People who influence or are influenced by the system or the other roles

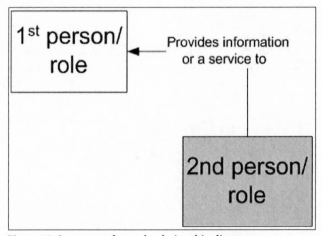

Figure 15: Structure of a work relationship diagram

The lines connect the roles indicating the information, goods, or services provided by one role to another. The arrow indicates the direction from producer to consumer. The rule is only one line between the same two roles. You can assume some reciprocation between roles so a corresponding return line and arrow is not needed. The WRD shows who is doing what for whom, not necessarily why they do it. We're assuming that the rewards are worth the effort and leave that problem for the why column. In Figure 15, let's assume person 2 mows the lawn for person 1. If person 1 pays person 2 then the diagram is correct; however, WRDs get interesting when we find that person 1 sends timesheets and quality reports to person 3 who sends a check to person 2. The WRD helps you identify work that happens under everyone's nose, but is rarely understood. Your WRD gets even more interesting if person 4 decides the annual bonus for person 2 and person 3 but not person 1.

Figure 16 shows a complete WRD for a real project. We often shade

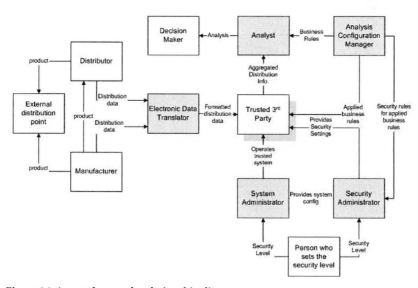

Figure 16: A complete work-relationship diagram

the boxes of the roles that interact directly with the system. There are two things of note here. First, the Decision Maker does not interact with the system; instead, an Analyst filters his information. Whether this is good or bad is impossible to tell, but knowing that the Analyst has to produce for a particular kind of consumer can help you build the right thing. Second, many arrows point to the Trusted 3rd Party. This role is clearly important and should receive the appropriate amount of attention during systems design.

Class/Data Model

Answers: What

Perspective: Logical

Data modeling, like process modeling, is a mature topic and the references are too numerous to list here. As with the process model, we don't have a modeling style preference. If you have never seen a data model (or a class diagram if you use object-oriented techniques), we have an example from a real project in Figure 17. Often

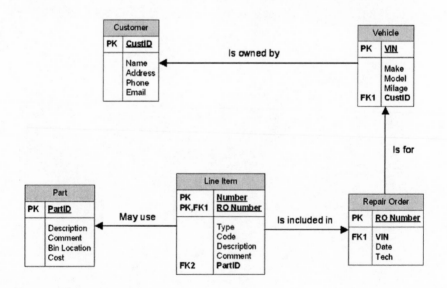

Figure 17: Data model example

data models are an excuse to overanalyze, so use them with caution. We prefer to only identify the high-level or critical classes or entities and leave the details for the design perspective.

Component Model

Answers: What (and sometimes a little bit of How)
Perspective: Logical

A component model is a high-level depiction of key system components. If you have ever attended a sales presentation for a

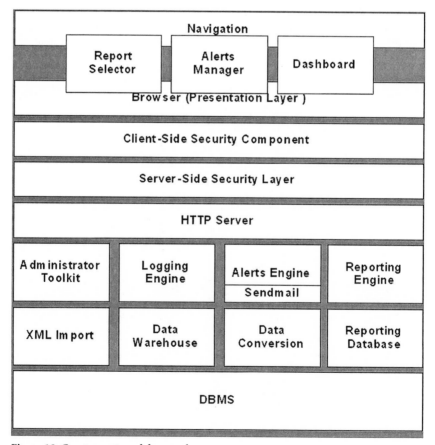

Figure 18: Component model example

complex commercial IT system, you have seen component models in one form or another because they are the only way to communicate system complexity in a way laymen can understand. A well-designed component model (and these are all more art than science) illustrates the overall architecture (e.g., layered, modular) and describes components where appropriate. I drew the component model shown in Figure 18 on the previous page for a project Russ was managing. After several attempts on the whiteboard, we redrew the final version in one corner so we could refer to it as we worked on other aspects of the systems design. It proved so useful that even a year later it had not been erased. I wouldn't be surprised to find new tenants in that building, but the component model still there.

Essential Use Case

Answers: Who and How (and sometimes What and Where)
Perspective: Logical

IT people who have experience in systems analysis and design probably have encountered one kind of use case or another. When we say essential use case, we very specifically mean the kind documented by Larry Constantine and Lucy Lockwood[19]. An essential use case describes a business (not technical) interaction between human and system. It is focused on the essentials of the business, not on things like routine error checking. A good set of essential use cases describes the lines on a context model and details the processes in your process model in a simple dialog between person and machine.

It is extremely important that your essential use cases are technology-agnostic. If you find the words click, scroll, tab, or the like in your essential use case, take them out and find a non-technical way

[19] Constantine, Larry and Lucy A. D. Lockwood. *Software For Use*. Boston: Addison Wesley Professional, 1999.

to describe what you mean. This exercise frees you from tech-bondage and you will be able to envision systems in new ways. Larry and Lucy's book has some great examples, but a simple one is the classic automated teller machine (ATM) where you want to get your money (actually you want to get mine, but we have agreed that the system will restrict such actions) from a bank where you have more than one account. Figure 19 shows how that would look.

ATM: Account Holder gets money	
User	**System**
1) Identify Self	
	2) Confirm Identity
3) Ask for Money	
	4) Which Account?
5) Choose Account	
	6) Give Money
7) Take Money	

Figure 19: Essential use case — Account holder gets money.

Good essential use cases take some practice even if the technique is simple. Start with a blank page. Write the name of the user role followed by the action they will take (Who does What). Draw a cross on the page and label the left side "User" and the right "System," then detail the essential steps of the business transaction. When you have a collection of essential use cases, you will find them useful not only as a logical description of the system, but also as test scripts and outlines for user training and documentation.

Technology Map

Answers: Where (and to some degree Who and What)
Perspective: Logical

As you move from the technology-agnostic essential use cases to deciding what you will need to physically implement your system, you must be conscious of the physical world. So much of IT systems is software, which can be a strictly mental exercise. But that software runs on some hardware and the hardware probably sits in a data center or on a customer's laptop. The technology map depicts technology choices on a map of the physical world. You can often begin with your context map (discussed earlier) to ensure you have covered the scope of the "where" that you care about.

On your technology map, identify your technology choices, or draw several maps if you have options. Document your network topology, indicating how information will move from one location to another. Still, remember that you are operating at the logical level and not the physical implementation. Although you are locating items in the physical world, keep the detail to the essential

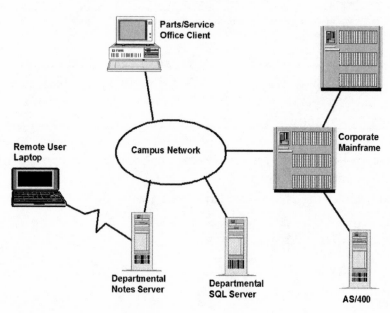

Figure 20: Technology map example

minimum, sufficient only to document and discuss your technology plan or options in the context of "where." We sometimes consider the component model (discussed earlier) a kind of technology map. Especially in systems where the whole thing resides in a single rack or even a single server, a component model can help depict the "where" of the essential components.

User Roles

Answers: Who
Context: Logical

Every system has several different types of users. The roles they play as part of the business purpose should have been identified in the work relationship diagram and context model. For each of these roles, briefly describe the role, how it is unique, the scope of the functions a person in that role performs, and what limits or restrictions should be levied on a person in that role. The short descriptions that follow are user roles for a case study we use in our training seminars:

Library Assistant – This person is responsible for day-to-day maintenance of the library and its assets. This role logs new books, records information on existing books, and helps customers find books. They also assist with the physical inventory and valuation process.

Chief Librarian – The Chief Librarian is ultimately responsible for the running of the library, and thus oversees all activities of the Library Assistant. The Chief Librarian performs physical inventories and valuation changes, and makes key decisions such as when/how assets are determined to be lost or should be disposed. They might also personally log/change asset information.

Customer – These are the staff who use the library. Customers come into the library to perform research, browse, and read as well as check-out/in assets. The check-out/in process requires library staff assistance, but users should be able to use the new system for online browsing.

Auditor – The auditor reviews the records of all assets, including the assets of the library. Specifically, the auditor is looking for recorded histories of all activities surrounding assets, particularly valuation changes. The Auditor also oversees how asset information pertaining to the library is entered into the accounting system.

Low-Fidelity Prototype (LFP)

Answers: What and How (and sometimes Where, Who, and When)

Perspective: Physical

The low-fidelity prototype (LFP) is literally a paper-and-pencil representation of the user interface of a software application. Each

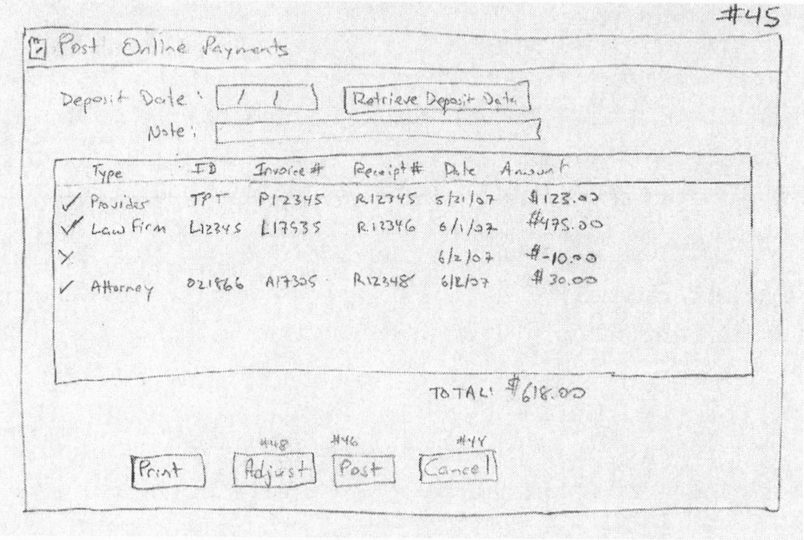

Figure 21: A portion of a low-fidelity prototype – page #45
Post On-Line Payments screen

piece of paper represents a screen or dialog window that would appear in the finished application. A LFP for an application might consist of 50 pieces of paper of varying sizes with hand-written labels, fields, and prompts. Notes are written on the back of each page to describe special features or functions on the screen. Pages are numbered for future reference.

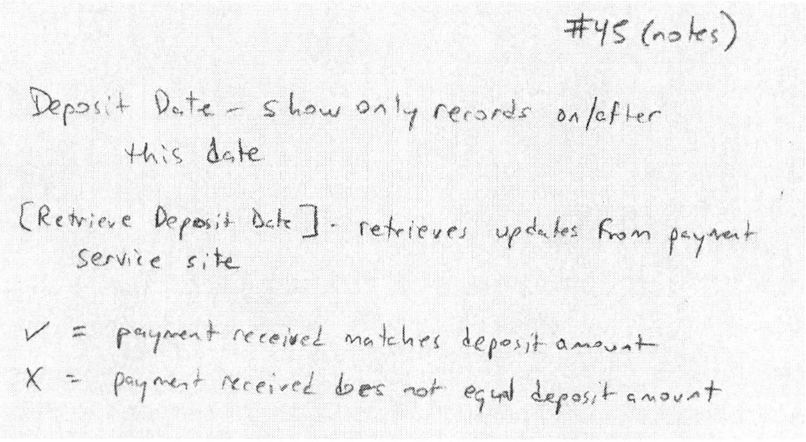

Figure 22: A portion of a low-fidelity prototype – back of page #45

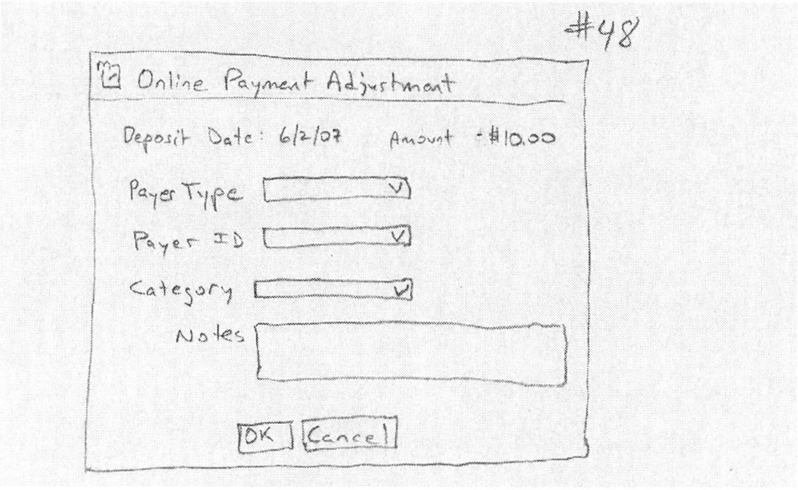

Figure 23: A portion of a low-fidelity prototype – page #48 Payment Adjustment dialog

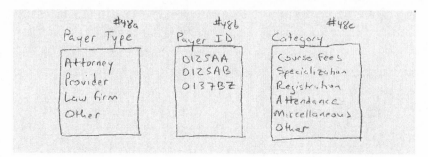

Figure 24: A portion of a low-fidelity prototype – page #48 drop-down lists

A LFP is not complete until it has been thoroughly tested. Using the essential use cases as scripts and the list of user roles to determine the test subjects, small groups (preferably pairs) of users are asked to test-drive the application. Using a pencil as their mouse and the pages of the LFP as the "screens," a user can very quickly test to see if the user interface works.

If the user finds a problem, they are encouraged to recommend changes or even make the change themselves. They are holding an eraser after all! The user interface will require changes, particularly with the first pairs of testers. If the first testers don't have any changes, then it is very likely that the wrong testers are involved. Once an LFP has gone through each test script successfully without changes, it can be considered complete.

Whole books could, and should, be written on the techniques for good low-fidelity prototyping because it is not as simple as it seems. The following examples give you some small idea of what can be done.

Interface Specification

Answers: How (and to a degree Who and What)
Perspective: Physical

The interface specification details the kinds of interface capability that will be necessary and the detailed specifications for system-to-system interaction. A common type of interface specification is XML where the data formats for system-to-system communication are specified. Interface specifications are as varied as the systems we use, so we won't provide an example. This is an area in which your IT people should be well versed. The main reason we include it in the matrix is to remind designers that interfaces have to be specified in order to be properly built. You leave the question of how they should be specified open to dangerous interpretation without an interface specification for each combination of system interactions.

Network Map

Answers: Where and What
Perspective: Physical

This diagram provides the details of the network architecture, identifying all essential components necessary for the operation of the application. These maps include devices, addresses, connections, configuration, and other information necessary to implement the items on the technology map and component model. A good network map doesn't fit well into a book of this size so, instead of a trivial example, we suggest you make your way to your local network administrator and ask to see a map of your existing network. If your firm is big enough to have a network administrator, you probably have a network map. You might wonder why we include it if one probably exists. We do this for two reasons: focus and change.

The map you will need for your application should only include those components necessary or affected by your system. This should give you a small enough map (depending on the scope of your system) to understand even if you are not a network engineer. Second, if your system proposes any changes to the current map or expects to add new pieces, your network engineers are going to need to see those in context so they can properly plan for the new capability.

Use-Case-to-Low-Fidelity-Prototype Map

Answers: Who
Context: Physical

The need for security and control will vary from system to system, but in the spirit of good governance (chapter 10) a use-case-to-low-fidelity-prototype map will help you maintain control of

Librarian Adds Book (1,2,3,4,6)	
User	**System**
1) I would like to add a book to the library.	
	2) Requests book info providing a structured way for the librarian to provide it
3) Provides book information: Title Dewey # Author Date Acquired Subject Condition Description Source Purchase Price Current Value	
4) Submits book information when satisfied it is complete and accurate.	
	5) Assigns a sequence #
	6) Saves book information and sequence number so it can be retrieved later.
	7) Updates a audit trail of book adds/changes
	8) Shows book details to librarian to prove the information has been properly stored.

Figure 25: Essential use case with LFP page mapping

the system from a testing, documentation, and security perspective. To create this map, simply indicate on the essential use cases the page numbers of the final low-fidelity prototype sheets that correspond with each step in the use case. This map will greatly assist in testing your prototype, but more importantly it tells you which user roles under which conditions (which process steps) will have access to or will need to understand which parts of the physical application. If you have properly marked your prototype with indications of the data needed, your database and security team can determine from the map the rules of access control for database and screen configuration.

Figure 25 shows a map from a simple use case from some of our training seminars. The numbers in the title are the prototype pages needed to complete this use case. On complex use cases, we might also add the numbers by the user or computer steps to help indicate which pages go with which steps. They should also be summarized together, as in the example, to prevent the team from hunting through pages of essential use cases to find the complete set of mappings.

Bibliography

Truly original works are rare, some would even say impossible. While this book contains some concepts we consider our own, most other aspects of our approach are adaptations, derivations or combinations of the best work of others. The following books are a small sample of what we consider the best reading in IT and business (relating to IT). As a general rule, any of the authors we have listed are worth reading even if we did not list one of their titles. Learn from us and then learn from these authors. You can always visit us at www.insightanthology.com to explore our current bibliography.

Joint Application Development

Wood, Jane and Denise Silver
John Wiley and Sons, 1994
ISBN: 0-471-04299-4

Good advice for managing analysis and design sessions and facilitation.

Zachman Framework for Enterprise Architecture

The Zachman Institute for Framework Advancement
Zachman, John and Samuel Holcman
www.zifa.com

This is the primary source of all information related to the Zachman Framework.

Peopleware: Productive Projects and Teams

DeMarco, Tom and Timothy Lister
Dorset House, 1987
ISBN: 0-932633-43-9

This is a must-read for all in the software development field.

Constantine on Peopleware

Constantine, Larry
Yourdon Press Computing Series, 1995
ISBN: 0133319768

Larry's practical observations about people are akin to Tom DeMarco and Tim Lister. He has an update called The Peopeware Papers which neither of us have read ... yet.

Software For Use

Constantine, Larry and Lucy A. D. Lockwood
Addison Wesley Professional, 1999
ISBN: 978-0201924787
http://www.foruse.com/

This is the definitive work on essential use cases (see appendix A) and a good read on overall systems design. Their articles and the resources on their website are outstanding. All of your designers should be familiar with Larry and Lucy's work.

The Mythical Man Month, Anniversary Edition

Brooks, Fredrick P. Jr.
Addison Wesley, 1995
ISBN: 0133319768

The original work was published in 1975, expanded in 1995, and is still relevant today.

The Art of Systems Architecting

Rechtin, Eberhardt and Mark W. Maier
CRC Press, 1997
ISBN: 0849304407

Read it for the heuristics. This is probably my favorite book on systems architecture.

The One Minute Methodology

Orr, Ken
Dorset House, 1990
ISBN: 0-932633-17-X

This very short, extremely funny book is another way of driving home the points we have made here.

Are your Lights On?

Weinberg, Gerald and Donald C. Gause
Dorset House, 1990
ISBN: 0-932633-16-1

Brief and inspiring, this book is a great introduction to thinking differently about systems problems. It contains the famous orange juice test (you'll have to read it yourself).

Exploring Requirements: Quality Before Design

Weinberg, Gerald and Donald C. Gause
Dorset House, 1990
ISBN: 0-932633-13-7

When it comes to thinking before you act, this book can help you avoid many errors in developing system requirements.

Handbook of Walkthroughs, Inspections, and Technical Reviews: Evaluating Programs, Projects, and Products, Third Edition

Freedman, Daniel P. and Gerald M. Weinberg

Dorset House, 1990

ISBN: 0-932633-19-6

This is the definitive guide on all forms of technical review. The principles are timeless and their explanations and experience are outstanding.

Quality Software Management, Vol. 2: First-Order Measurement

Weinberg, Gerald M.

Dorset House, 1993

ISBN: 0-932633-24-2

Weinberg is probably the premier systems thinker and develops excellent examples to help you think differently about systems problems.

Essential Systems Analysis

McMenamin, Stephen M. and John F. Palmer

Prentice-Hall, 1984

ISBN: 0-917072-30-8

The classic work on reducing systems analysis to its essence. Last we checked, this was out of print, but it is a worthwhile read if you can find it.

Why Does Software Cost So Much?
(And Other Puzzles of the Information Age)

DeMarco, Tom
Dorset House, 1995
ISBN: 0-932633-34-X

A fun set of essays on a variety of topics pertaining to systems and information. Particularly useful is the essay on the cost of software.

The Deadline

DeMarco, Tom
Dorset House, 1997
ISBN: 0-932633-39-0
www.systemsguild.com

This novel is the most fun you will ever have with project management. A must-read.

A Timeless Way of Building

Alexander, Christopher
Oxford University Press, 1979
ISBN: 0-19-502402-8

Mr. Alexander is not a technologist, he's a practicing architect and builder. This a great and unique book for stepping above the technological fray and trying to understand how people think, feel, and communicate about how the things around them are and should be designed, built, and given life.

Facilitator's Guide to Participatory Decision-Making

Kaner, Sam, et. al.,
New Society Publishers, 1996
ISBN: 0-86571-347-2

Good basic work on facilitation. Will help develop greater communication and exploratory skills.

Good to Great

Collins, Jim
Harper Business, 2001
ISBN: 9780066620992

Interesting reading about what makes corporations great. I particularly like the hedgehog concept (a corporate-level business purpose in a nutshell).

The 4-Hour Workweek

Ferriss, Timothy
Crown Publishing, 2007
ISBN: 9780307353139

Admittedly, this author can be a little over-the-top and obviously has a very short attention span; however, he has some great points about work-life balance and will certainly make you nervous about the mindset of the next generation of workers.

The Discipline of Market Leaders

Treacy, Michael and Fred Wiersema
Basic Books Publishing, 1997
ISBN: 201407191

A now classic business text, the key point for our readers is you can't do it all. Pick something and do that. Watch out for business purposes that are impossible to achieve. This book can help you see one way to focus.

About the Authors

Steve Caudill

Steve Caudill is a senior IT manager at PepsiCo International acting as the functional lead of the worldwide direct-store-delivery business for a global SAP implementation. His career journey has included the roles of soldier, spy, consultant, entrepreneur, technology researcher, writer, editor, speaker, and general troublemaker. He loves really complex problems particularly related to people and international business issues. You can reach him at smcaudill5@gmail.com.

Russell Mullen
www.dacoda.us

Russell Mullen is Principal Consultant of Dacoda Projects LLC. Over twenty years in IT doing everything from development, to team management, to administration, he's had plenty of opportunity to find easier ways to overcome hard problems. He specializes in providing expert project management and design consulting services, ensuring that the project teams deliver to customers what they expect, that risks are addressed so that those projects stay on-time and on-budget, and that communication is open, effective, consistent, and well-managed. You can reach him at rmullen@dacoda.us.